2-18-75

CAREER GUIDANCE
FOR YOUNG WOMEN

Publication No. 950

AMERICAN LECTURE SERIES

A Publication in

The BANNERSTONE DIVISION *of* AMERICAN LECTURES
IN SOCIAL AND REHABILITATION PSYCHOLOGY

Editors of the Series

JOHN G. CULL, Ph.D.
Director, Regional Counselor Training Program
Department of Rehabilitation Counseling
Virginia Commonwealth University
Fisherville, Virginia

RICHARD E. HARDY, Ed.D.
Diplomate in Counseling Psychology
and
Chairman, Department of Rehabilitation Counseling
Virginia Commonwealth University
Richmond, Virginia

The American Lecture Series in Social and Rehabilitation Psychology offers books which are concerned with man's role in his milieu. Emphasis is placed on how this role can be made more effective in a time of social conflict and a deteriorating physical environment. The books are oriented toward descriptions of what future roles should be and are not concerned exclusively with the delineation and definition of contemporary behavior. Contributors are concerned to a considerable extent with prediction through the use of a functional view of man as opposed to a descriptive, anatomical point of view.

Books in this series are written mainly for the professional practitioner; however, academicians will find them of considerable value in both undergraduate and graduate courses in the helping services.

CAREER GUIDANCE
FOR YOUNG WOMEN

Considerations in Planning
Professional Careers

Edited by

RICHARD E. HARDY, Ed.D.

Diplomate in Counseling Psychology

JOHN G. CULL, Ph.D.

C H A R L E S   C   T H O M A S   ·   P U B L I S H E R
Springfield   ·   Illinois   ·   U.S.A.

Published and Distributed Throughout the World by
CHARLES C THOMAS • PUBLISHER
BANNERSTONE HOUSE
301-327 East Lawrence Avenue, Springfield, Illinois, U.S.A.

© *1974, by* CHARLES C THOMAS • PUBLISHER
ISBN 0-398 03139-8 (cloth)
ISBN 0-398 03140-1 (paper)
Library of Congress Catalog Card Number: 74-1033

With THOMAS BOOKS *careful attention is given to all details of manufacturing and design. It is the publisher's desire to present books that are satisfactory as to their physical qualities and artistic possibilities and appropriate for their particular use.* THOMAS BOOKS *will be true to those laws of quality that assure a good name and good will.*

Printed in the United States of America
N-1

Library of Congress Cataloging in Publication Data

Hardy, Richard E
    Career guidance for young women.

    (American lecture series, publication no. 950. A publication in the Bannerstone division of American lectures in social and rehabilitation psychology)
    1. Vocational guidance for women—Addresses, essays, lectures. I. Cull, John G., joint author. II. Title.
HF5381.H138   331.7'02   74-1033
ISBN 0-398-03139-8
ISBN 0-398-03140-1 (pbk.)

CONTRIBUTORS

GWENDOLYN H. AUSTIN is an Education Program Specialist in the U. S. Office of Education, Washington, D. C. Prior to this position she was a school officer in the D. C. public school system where she had been employed as a teacher for eighteen years. She has conducted numerous workshops in curriculum development for urban areas and is currently completing requirement for the Ed. D. Degree in Urban Education.

DOROTHY B. FLOYD is a school counselor in the Charlotte-Mecklenburg Schools. She resides in Charlotte, North Carolina. Her educational background includes a B.S. Degree in Home Economics from Shaw University, an M.S. Degree in Education from North Carolina A&T University, and an M.A. equivalent degree in Guidance from the Atlanta University. She has done postbaccalaureate study at the University of Louisville, University of North Carolina, Meredith College, North Carolina State University, Appalachian State University, and University of Maine. Formerly she was a teacher of World War II veterans and a classroom teacher in public schools in North Carolina. She was a part-time instructor of adolescent psychology at Johnson C Smith University. Mrs. Floyd is quite active in professional affairs and is listed in several biographical reference works.

GRACE H. FOSTER is Corporate Secretary of the Central Bank of Oakland, California. Mrs. Foster has held many of the jobs available in banking systems which females traditionally hold. She has over twenty years of experience in banking.

EVELYN STAPLES GRINDLE is an ordained minister of the United Methodist Church presently serving churches in Wilton and North Jay in Franklin County, Maine. Previously Mrs. Grindle served Methodist churches in Penobscot, Brooksville, Elsworth, Surry, Trenton (Union), Winterport and Wayne. She was born in Penobscot, Maine, taught public school in Warren and Verona. She is the widow of Shirley H. Grindle, and mother of an adopted son and daughter. Mrs. Grindle has nine grandchildren and is past president of the New England Association of Women Ministers and past Corresponding Secretary of the American Association of Women Ministers (now an International Association).

CECILY ANNE GARDNER GRUMBINE, Ph.D., is director of the Counseling Service of the University of North Colorado, Greely, Colorado. Her areas of specialty include psychotherapy, psychodiagnostics, and clinical child psychology. She is active in group therapy which includes the techniques of encounter-groups, sensitivity training and T-Groups. Part of her practice of psychology includes marriage and family counseling and personality assessment. Dr. Grumbine received her doctorate in Psychology from the University of Chicago. She is licensed as a psychologist in Colorado and Illinois. Formerly she was a geriatic psychologist at the Fort Logan Mental Health Center in Denver and was a psychologist with the Counseling Service of Greeley, Colorado. She has been the Dean of Women and an Assistant Professor of Psychology at the University of Northern Colorado.

BETTY L. GRUNDY, M.D., is a Fellow of the American College of Anesthesiologist and a Diplomate of the American Board of Anesthesiologists, Dr. Grundy was born in Dothan, Alabama and received her medical training at the University of Florida, College of Medicine. She is presently chairman of the Anesthesiologist Department at St. Luke's Hospital in Saginaw, Michigan. She has been an anesthesiologist in Saginaw, Michigan since 1967. Prior to that she was in general practice in South Dakota.

VIRGINIA LEE McKEMIE-BELT, Ph.D., is vice-president for finance of the Open "A" Company, Inc., on leave from the University of California. Dr. McKemie-Belt received her Ph.D. in Business Finance from the University of Illinois. She has been a professor at the University of Illinois, California State College, and the University of California. She is President of Financial Programming, Inc.; public lecturer, Illinois Banker Association; public lecturer, Insurance Institute of America and others. She is an economic consultant for the California Resources Development and the Illinois Council on Economic Education. She has published extensively in the area of business, finance and economics.

BETTY MURDOCK, Ph.D., was born in Webb City, Missouri. She holds a B.S. degree from Kansas State College of Pittsburg, an M.A. degree from Washington State University in Pullman, and a Ph.D. degree from the University of Missouri. Dr. Murdock's teaching career includes positions with the public schools in Galena, Kansas; Pullman, Washington; Independence, Oregon; Five Points and San Jose, California. During her tenure at Pullman, Washington, she also supervised student teachers for Washington State University. Since 1960 she has been a speech correctionist in the Milpitas Unified School District, Milpitas, California, where she also supervises student therapists from San Jose State University. She is active in the Milpitas Education Association having twice held office as president. She is a representative to the State Council of Education of the California Teachers Association and equal rights chairman of its State Human Relations Committee. She holds a certificate of Clinical Competence in Speech Pathology from the American Speech and Hearing Association. She is also a member of the California Speech and Hearing Association and a life member of the National Education Association. Honorary memberships include Phi Kappa Phi, Pi Kappa Delta, Kappa Delta Pi and Theta Alpha Phi. Dr. Murdock also is listed in several biographical reference works.

PRESTON M. ROYSTER is the acting Director of Community Education, Teacher Corps, U.S. Office of Education, Washington, D.C. Prior to this position he served as Acting Director of Teacher Corps. He also served in the Bureau of Equal Educational Opportunity and as director of Equal Employment Opportunity. Both of these positions and previous volunteer community activities required that Dr. Royster give career counseling to many students and employees. He conducted an extensive study of the displacement of black educators and published his findings on this topic.

MARGARET BELAIS SALMON, M.S., is Chief Dietician at St. Joseph's Hospital in Paterson, New Jersey; Nutrition Consultant at various schools, hospitals, and nursing homes; and a lecturer at the Passaic Community College. Mrs. Salmon received her B.S. in Food Chemistry Nutrition and Dietetic at the University of California in Berkeley, and her M.S. in Nutrition Education at Columbia University. She is Editor of *Enjoying Your Restricted Diet* and author of *Food Facts for Teenagers* both of which were published by Charles C Thomas, Publisher.

BEATRICE L. SHEPARD is a Microbiologist. She is the Regional Laboratory Supervisor, South Eastern Regional Laboratory of the Alaska Department of Health and Social Services, Juneau, Alaska. Formerly she was Director of Riverside County Public Health Laboratory, Riverside, California; Public Health Chemist for a Los Angeles County; Public Health Chemist for the State of Alaska, Department of Health; Acting Chief, Section of Public Health Laboratories, Alaska Department of Health and Social Services. She is a member of the American Society for Microbiologists, The American Institute of Biological Sciences, and the American Association for the Advancement of Science. Ms. Shepard has for many years been interested in developing programs for the active recruitment of young people for various scientific specialties.

BRADLEY SOULE, M.D., was formerly a research associate at the National Institutes of Health. He is now with the Overholzer Training and Research Division, Saint Elizabeth's Hospital, Washington, D.C.

KAY STANDLEY, Ph.D., is with the Social and Behavioral Sciences Branch of the National Institute of Child Health and Human Development, National Institutes of Health, United States Department of Health, Education and Welfare, Bethesda, Maryland.

*Books that have appeared thus far in the Social and Rehabilitation
Psychology series:*

VOCATIONAL ADJUSTMENT: THE GOAL OF REHABILITATION
John G. Cull and Richard E. Hardy

GROUP COUNSELING IN SPECIAL SETTINGS
Richard E. Hardy and John G. Cull

TYPES OF DRUG ABUSERS AND THEIR ABUSES
John G. Cull and Richard E. Hardy

DRUG DEPENDENCE AND REHABILITATION APPROACHES
Richard E. Hardy and John G. Cull

ORGANIZATION AND ADMINISTRATION OF DRUG ABUSE TREATMENT
PROGRAMS
John G. Cull and Richard E. Hardy

CLIMBING GHETTO WALLS
Richard E. Hardy and John G. Cull

REHABILITATION OF THE URBAN DISADVANTAGED
John G. Cull and Richard E. Hardy

EDUCATIONAL AND PSYCHOLOGICAL ASPECTS OF DEAFNESS
Richard E. Hardy and John G. Cull

VOCATIONAL REHABILITATION: PROFESSION AND PROCESS
John G. Cull and Richard E. Hardy

MEDICAL AND PSYCHOLOGICAL ASPECTS OF DISABILITY
A. Beatrix Cobb

This book is dedicated to an outstanding professional person, Miss Margaret M. Ryan, Rehabilitation Services administration, Department of Health, Education and Welfare, Washington, D.C., whose accomplishments are well known to many professional individuals and clients alike in the fields of rehabilitation and social work.

PREFACE

W E, THE EDITORS, are delighted at the completion of this career guidance text which we feel will be of considerable value to young women who are evaluating whether or not to enter professional training at either the college level or graduate level. The persons selected as contributors to this book are outstanding women and men who have achieved high professional status.

We feel that their candid and practical approach to describing opportunities, barriers, problems and solutions in reference to their specific career area offers considerable possibilities for generalization to related professions. This is a book written for the most part by women for the use of young women and those who attempt to provide counseling and job advice. In this volume the editors deserve credit only for planning, coordination and final integration of materials.

While we have varied from the professional jargon somewhat in the use of the words "occupation" and "career," we have done so out of personal preference. The reader may wish to keep in mind that "career" is often defined in the professional jargon as a sequence of occupations, jobs, and positions engaged in by a person throughout his lifetime. In the title of this book we have used the term "career" as if it were synonomous with "occupation."

Without the high level of interest exhibited by the contributors, the development of this book would have been impossible. We owe to each of them any degree of success which may come from the use of the book in counseling settings and individual job exploration.

RICHARD E. HARDY
JOHN G. CULL

Richmond, Virginia

xiii

CONTENTS

		Page
Contributors	....	v
Preface	....	xiii

Chapter

1. WOMEN IN PROFESSIONS: Historic Antecedents and Current Lifestyles—*Kay Standley, Ph.D. and Bradley Soule, M.D.* ... 3
2. CAREER ROLES IN MEDICINE—*Betty L. Grundy* 17
3. CAREER ROLES IN DIETETICS—*Margaret Belais Salmon* 27
4. THE WOMEN IN THE BUSINESS OF ECONOMICS—*Virginia Lee McKemie-Belt* 50
5. BANKING AS A CAREER AREA FOR WOMEN—*Grace H. Foster* .. 64
6. CAREER ROLES IN THE MINISTRY—*Evelyn Staples Grindle* ... 75
7. CAREER ROLES IN SPEECH THERAPY—*Betty Murdock* 101
8. CAREER ROLES FOR FEMALES IN PSYCHOLOGY—*Cecily Grumbine* 112
9. TEACHING IN SECONDARY AND ELEMENTARY SCHOOLS— *Gwendolyn H. Austin* 132
10. SEX DISCRIMINATION IN EDUCATION: AN OVERVIEW 147
11. CAREER ROLES IN GUIDANCE COUNSELING—*Dorothy B. Floyd*.. 170
12. CAREER ROLES FOR FEMALES IN PHYSICAL SCIENCES— *Beatrice L. Shepard* 192

Index 205

CAREER GUIDANCE
FOR YOUNG WOMEN

CHAPTER 1

WOMEN IN PROFESSIONS: HISTORIC ANTECEDENTS AND CURRENT LIFESTYLES[1]

KAY STANDLEY, PH.D. AND BRADLEY SOULE, M.D.

//

Methodology

Results

References

//

ENCOURAGED BY PROMISES of government officialdom and goaded by feminist rhetoric, working women and women who want to work look forward to a revolution in women's roles. There are clear indications that career women and their occupational worlds are changing, but the nature of these shifts is not well-defined. The confusion of the social scientists' prognostications reflects society's muddled evaluation of the feminist movement.

It is no simple matter to examine such change in historical terms, for the vocational development of women has been a subject of systematic inquiry only within the last several years. Attempts to formulate theories of vocational choice appropriate to women are meager (Psathas, 1968). Rather, much of the work in the field has sought to contradict the folklore, documenting that trained women are in fact productive but are discriminated against in their careers.

---

[1]This paper is a revised version of a paper presented by the authors at the annual meeting of the American Psychological Association in Hawaii, 1972.

A 1963 *Business Week* article justified its advocacy of equality with the title, "On the Job, Women Act Much Like Men," and looked for facts "beyond the anecdotes about the president's secretary who is such a treasure, and about that snip in the typing pool who used up all her sick leave and quit" (p. 114).

Within the professions, Shapiro (1968) and Williams (1971) have surveyed the careers of physicians; White (1967) and Epstein (1971) have discussed women in the law; and Astin (1969) has reported on the woman doctorate. With the exception of Epstein's work, these studies relied on questionnaire data for information on work experiences and current family situations with only brief excursions into the earlier personal and social histories of their subjects.

Although a number of investigators have studied the personal characteristics of college and career women, reports on the personalities of successful professionals have been rare. Bachtold and Werner (1970) have presented "Personality Profiles of Women Psychologists" in terms of responses to the Sixteen PF Questionnaire, and Cartwright (1972) has used a family history schedule in addition to objective measures of the personalities of women medical students. Helson (1966) has reported more extensive data on a broader sample of creative women.

Some current work focuses on the particular problems of the woman professional who chooses to combine family and career roles. While the studies of the Rapoports (1971) in England sample a range of work orientations of married women, Epstein (1971) and Hoffman (1972) point to the special incongruities of housewifery and motherhood on the one hand and the pursuit of a professional career on the other. Within each profession there are calls for training programs and employment situations which would facilitate the careers of women with family responsibilities. Kaplan's (1970) report on the recruitment and utilization of women physicians is one such presentation.

Many of the unresolved issues about women professionals cluster around two major questions. What are the roots of their unusual choices? What are the careers and personal lives like for the women who have made such vocational commitments?

This research project, then, is an effort to delineate certain aspects of the personal and career histories of some women physicians, lawyers and architects. It is a portrayal of women who have faced extreme contradictions of social roles by seeking to enter the male-dominated establishments of high-status professions. The study was undertaken in the hope that an understanding of such conflicts and of the personalities which coped with them would speak to the issues of the future—as well as the current—work of women.

METHODOLOGY

Subjects

Eighty women in medicine, law and architecture were recruited for the study through telephone contacts. They ranged in age from twenty-four to sixty years with a mean age of thirty-five. The core sample was based on the directories of the appropriate professional organizations and was supplemented through personal contacts to include a more complete range of ages and work experiences. The sample was not intended to reflect demographic characteristics of the full population of women professionals as would be required for a survey; it was rather composed of women practicing in a wide variety of professional settings in the East, primarily the Washington, D.C., area.

Criteria for selection were (1) working at least half-time in a position appropriate to the profession; (2) having obtained the professional academic degree (M.D., LL.B., or B.Arch.) at least one year previously; (3) being United States born and academically trained; and (4) Caucasian.

Procedures

All subjects completed a questionnaire devised by the investigators[2] and in almost all cases were interviewed at length by the investigators conjointly. Both questionnaire and interview focused on aspects of childhood which seemed particularly relevant to the development of motivations, interests and attitudes about work: (1) childhood activities, aspirations, and relationships with peers and

---

[2]Some questionnaire items are based on the survey of women doctorates by Astin (1969) and the forms used by Turner and Turner (1971).

(2) parental characteristics and values, especially with regard to the academic accomplishment of their daughters and the work of women. In addition, a number of the variables under study related to the courses of these women's professional careers and their current lifestyles.

The interviews were open-ended in that the woman was encouraged to discuss any aspect of her history which she thought was important to her career, but the interviewers also directed her attention to the same dimensions covered by the questionnaire.

The questionnaire asked for a wide range of biographical information and ratings of certain attitudes and values—of the subjects, their parents, and if married, their husbands. In view of the descriptive purpose of the study, the form intentionally covered a large number of dimensions suggested by the literature on vocational development and academic success. Specifically, it included the following areas: (1) background variables such as age, place of birth, siblings, and ethnicity; (2) parental characteristics (education, occupations, ages and incomes as well as personal descriptions), evaluation of the subject's relationships with them, parental attitudes about maternal work, and parental child rearing practices and values; (3) social development (childhood activities, peer relationships, dating history) and current social and professional relationships with men and other women; and (4) career development (the time of vocational decision and influences on it, education and training, parental attitudes about the subject's education and work) and perceptions of sex discrimination in her profession.

RESULTS

The results presented here are based on percentages of responses to questionnaire items. This summary includes the data for the total group of women professionals, although a few striking differences among the physicians, lawyers and architects are noted. Some initial results from a professional male sample are contrasted with the female group. (Data from a comparison group of females—matched for socioeconomic background and educational attainment, but in traditional female roles—are currently being gathered.)

Historical Factors

The families of origin of the women professionals are decidedly upper middle class and professional in a number of respects. Over half of the fathers are reported to have had incomes above $15,000 annually, 32 percent above $25,000, and 58 percent are employed in high status professions. These data support Williams' (1971) conclusion that Radcliffe alumni who entered medicine represented an urban, affluent, educated and professional milieu. Likewise, Cartwright's (1972) sample of California female medical students reflected the same background of paternal educational and occupational accomplishment. In contrast, the male sample of the present study came from somewhat lower socioeconomic status homes: only 30 percent of their fathers had earned more than $15,000 and 27 percent were professionals.

Family ethnicity of the sample was reported as 58 percent WASP, 23 percent Jewish, and 19 percent other (mostly Eastern European extraction). A high proportion of parents were foreign-born, but not as high as in Astin's (1969) group of women doctorates. In this sample, 20 percent of the fathers and 11 percent of the mothers were foreign born.

Mothers of the women professionals tended to be well-educated (20% had attended graduate school), but 43 percent of them never worked after they had children. Of those who did work, however, 42 percent worked full-time for at least ten years during the subjects' childhoods. Furthermore, even though 76 percent of these workers never earned more than $10,000 annually, a majority (61%) of the subjects thought their mothers enjoyed their work. Seventy-one percent also felt that their fathers were pleased with their mothers' working. In the professional male sample, 61 percent of the mothers never worked, but of those who did 72 percent are thought to have enjoyed it. However, only 31 percent of the fathers in these families were thought to have approved of their wives' working. Comparison of the two groups, then, suggests that the mothers of women professionals are more likely to have worked and with the approval of their husbands but were not as pleased with working or with their jobs.

Interpretation of these findings is naturally troubled by problems of retrospective bias: one wonders if women professionals need to "justify" their careers with parental (especially paternal) acceptance of women's working. Clearly the women report a family appreciation of working women. Baruch (1972) contends that not merely the fact of maternal employment but also the attitude toward it is crucial in a young woman's valuation of feminine competence.

Fifty-four percent of the women professionals are only or oldest children, and 63 percent are the only or oldest females of their siblings. These figures are only slightly higher than those for men in the study: 49 percent of the men were only or oldest children, and 60 percent hold that position among male siblings only—comparable to Coker's (1959) data on the birth order of a sample of (mostly male) medical students. The importance of early-born status in all highly educated groups has been well-documented (Schachter, 1963).

In addition to demographic information, the data also described aspects of the early psychosocial environments of the subjects. In interviews, the women gave vivid accounts of their parents' preoccupations with academic achievement and assumptions of excellence in their daughters. On the questionnaire the subjects were asked to select three from a list of qualities which had been "encouraged by parents." Eighty-eight per cent of the women selected items relating to achievement: "making good grades," "acting responsibly," "having self-discipline," and "being intellectually curious." Few women felt that their parents had stressed affectionate behavior, social skills, sex-appropriate behavior, or "neatness," more traditional expectations of young females. Not surprisingly, these choices of qualities valued by parents were directly paralleled in the male sample. At this point, it is not clear whether these same values are common to most families or are peculiar to parents of professionals; the crucial comparison will be with educated women who do not work.

Correspondingly, the women report on the questionnaire that of social, moral, intellectual and physical characteristics, their parents mostly highly valued their daughters' intellectual attributes. Table 1-I indicates that the women concur in terms of what quality they most like about themselves and overwhelmingly rate their physical characteristics as least valued. The men professionals showed similar rankings.

TABLE 1-I.
RANKINGS OF VALUED PERSONAL ATTRIBUTES

Questionnaire item	social	moral	Intellectual	Physical
What quality does your father like most about you?	8%	16%	73%	3%
What quality does your mother . . .	24%	24%	52%	0%
What quality do you like most about yourself?	15%	30%	54%	1%
What quality do you like least about yourself?	28%	10%	1%	61%

How did these women spend their time as children? The subjects were asked to recall whether they found various childhood activities very pleasurable, moderately so, or not at all pleasurable. A number of responses contradicted traditional notions of usual and appropriate feminine play: 57 percent of the women noted greater enjoyment of active "tomboyish" activities such as climbing trees and playing with boys as compared with 34 percent who said they found greater pleasure in sewing, cooking, helping their mothers around the house, or organizing the play of younger children (9% gave no preference to either group of activities). One wonders if these girls who grew up to enter occupationally masculine worlds did express themselves in play which was different from their peers, or if, in fact, the traditional assumptions about sex-typed play preference are fallacious.

In later adolescent years, the women were not socially active. Over one quarter of the sample (42% of the physicians) never dated at all. (Nineteen % of the men never dated in high school.) From interviews an impression emerged of solitary intellectual and artistic pursuits during adolescence. An "ugly duckling" theme was common, the women recalled years of social incompetence, loneliness and generally low self-esteem. Most experienced college and professional training years as periods of social awakening.

It seems that parents encouraged the beginnings of autonomy and achievement, but there is evidence that many did not expect their daughters to embrace such values and behaviors so completely. While the subjects' perceptions of what parental reactions would have been if they had dropped out of professional school stressed parental disappointment (72% for the fathers and 61% for the mothers), the parents were clearly thought to be more ambivalent or even pleased at the prospect of their daughters' quitting their work at present. The subjects reported that only 25 percent of their mothers and 40 percent of their fathers would be disappointed if they dropped their careers. In one interview, one woman physician noted the full support her family had given her academic endeavors and then her surprise when, upon graduation from medical school, her parents urged her not to practice.

Correspondingly, nearly all the women thought that their mothers wanted them to be married and have children, and in the majority of instances to limit their careers (69%). However, 18 percent of the women report that at sixteen years of age they expected to have careers without husbands or children and another 35 percent expected full-time careers with families. In actuality, some of the daughters (29%) did incorporate their parents' ambivalence and spun from it a dual role model of full-time career and family life; others are not married or do not work full-time.

The women's reports of their childhood and current relationships with their parents support inference from interview material: while the professionals profess to intimate, influential relationships with their fathers, it was in fact their mothers who primarily motivated and guided them toward nontraditional behaviors, attitudes and careers choices. Eighty-one percent stated that they were by father's favorite, but only 33 per cent felt that they were favored by their mother. When asked which parent they respect the most, 66 percent of those who made a choice named their fathers compared with 34 percent for mothers. But it was the mothers to whom they confided (79% versus 21% for fathers), who influenced how they spent their spare time (76% versus 24%), and whom they need most now (74% for mothers and 26% for fathers). The fathers of the women professionals may have indeed provided the role model of academic success and social status, but the mothers—described by almost half of the sample as competent, bright, warm and active —encouraged their daughters to obtain social recognition for paternal rather than maternal roles. Thus while the family patterns of most of the sample were of the classic patriarchal type (the father as "king" and the mother the "power behind the throne") there seems evidence of a peculiar brand of court ideology which offered high encouragement to the daughters to achieve in traditionally masculine spheres. The dynamics behind this pattern must remain speculative, but some of the interview material suggested the hypothesis that the mothers of the professional women were themselves vocationally and socially frustrated women who trained their daughters for another course of economic gain and social recognition. Deeply ambivalent about their daughters' careers, they seemed themselves (viewed retrospectively through the interview) to have been ambivalent as well about the limits which traditional sex roles had placed upon their own achievement. There are indications that the mothers were as competent, bright and ambitious as the fathers, but unfulfilled in their realization of these qualities.

With this parental encouragement in childhood, a number of the future professionals, especially the physicians, first considered their careers at an early age. Table 1-II shows that these career decisions were being considered at an earlier age than in the male professional sample, although the final choices were made at similar times in the two groups.

Surprisingly few of the women seriously considered careers other than the ones they finally chose. When alternative choices did exist, the other occupations were primarily in related disciplines

TABLE 1-II.
TIME OF CAREER DECISIONS: FIRST CONSIDERED
CURRENT CAREER AND FINALLY DECIDED IN CAREER

| | WOMEN | | | | | | | | MEN | |
| TIME OF DECISION | *Physicians* | | *Lawyers* | | *Architects* | | *All Women* | | | |
	first	final	first	final	first	final	first	final	first	final
Elementary School	46%	7%	19%	8%	24%	12%	30%	9%	15%	6%
High School	35	30	19	13	28	23	27	21	55	25
College	19	44	52	46	40	46	36	46	23	48
After College	0	18	10	33	8	19	7	24	7	20

Note—Percentages in a column may not add to 100 percent due to decimals.

rather than in another field of similar status. About one quarter of the architects, for example, considered careers in art, and a comparable percentage of physicians thought of entering nursing or a scientific career. In general, however, these women seemed to pursue their career goals in a single direction; one suspects that it was important to their vocational development to be specific and unswerving in their plans in order to convince others of their seriousness.

Current Careers and Life-styles

Seventy-two per cent of the sample of women are or have been married, and the largest percentage of these were married after obtaining a professional degree: 27 percent after college but before graduate school, 25 percent married during professional school, and 43 percent after completing professional training. The times of the men's marriages are almost identical with the exception that none married in an interim period between college and professional school, a common happening in the women's lives.

Almost all (93%) of the women's husbands are professionals themselves: 100 percent of the lawyers, 86 percent of the physicians, and 94 percent of the architects are married to professionals. About two thirds of these marriages are to mates in the same profession. Since most of the women married when they were well on their way to becoming professionals and since their professional husbands well understood the rigors of such careers, it is surprising that 42 percent of the women reported that their husbands would be pleased or at least ambivalent (pleased in some ways but displeased in others) over the prospect of their quitting work.

In spite of the "richness of commitments," as Hoffman (1972) speaks of it, to the several roles of wife, mother and professional, the interviews were replete with tales of the agonies common to these women. A number spoke of the different "personalities'" they present at work and at home, and for many the inherent psychic conflicts make for difficult coping—especially the younger ones who are perhaps not yet comfortable with their professional or marital identities.

> Although these professional women (physicians) behave in a way that
> bears out their feeling that they should not completely sacrifice their

personal goals, they accept that a woman should sacrifice her personal goals for the sake of the family, and should make these sacrifices more than men.

(Steinman, *et al.,* 1964)

The women find severe contradictions in the expectations made of them at home and work. At work, some of the women apparently resolve the active-passive dilemma by being especially assertive and authoritarian, but the vast majority seem to place themselves in subservient or "service" positions to male colleagues, e.g. functioning primarily as a consultant. At home, the married women professionals clearly assume most of the traditional tasks of housewife and mother, however much they may extoll the virtues of their helping husbands or insist that household management is an egalitarian arrangement. When a child is sick, for example, it is almost invariably the woman who stays home from work. The vocational requirements of a husband's career have likewise shown clear precedence over the wife's during the course of the marriage. Moves have usually been occasioned by a brighter job prospect for the husband with the wife's "finding a good position" in the new setting.

How do these women perceive their profession now that they are practicing? What are their perceptions of how women professionals fare? One-third have found that there are some aspects of professional practice which pose difficulties for them because of their sex. In architecture, this is on-site supervision of construction; in law, it is courtroom activity; and in medicine, the bastion of masculinity is the operating room.

Table 1-III shows the percentage of the male and female samples who feel that there is discrimination against women in certain aspects of their professions. Both women and men indicate relatively less discrimination in achievement evaluation in professional school, although the male professionals in general tend to perceive less discrimination than do the females. One notable exception is acceptance by peers: perhaps women think that their male colleagues accept them as equals, but the men know better!

There is some indication of the toll that these nontraditional courses of vocational and family lives have taken on these women.

TABLE 1-III.

PERCEPTIONS OF DISCRIMINATION AGAINST WOMEN IN OWN PROFESSION

AREAS OF DISCRIMINATION	WOMEN				MEN
	Physicians	*Lawyers*	*Architects*	*All Women*	
Admission to profession	62%	48%	42%	51%	37%
Peer acceptance	39	60	39	47	63
Achievement evaluation by professors	19	20	27	23	19
Acceptance by clients or patients	31	72	50	52	57
Employer practices in hiring and salaries	39	88	65	65	55
Promotion and advancement	46	80	69	66	57
"I do not feel that there is undue discrimination" (no other items checked)	27	8	41	22	27

Note — The columns of percentages do not total 100 percent since respondents could mark any number of items.

While it seems that all professionals, men and women, feel that their lives have been particularly stressful, women especially (65%) indicated that they have had very difficult periods in their lives or that they feel they are frequently "skating on thin ice." Sixty-two percent of the female sample have had psychiatric treatment.

The joys of professional attainment are also evident in the women, if tempered by the stress and discrimination. One would suspect that their satisfactions are in some respects similar to those of the men: the fulfillment of academic and occupational success. Beyond that, for many women lies the pride in having achieved what few have done successfully—to gain entry to and function in an elite male-typed vocation. As they state the pleasure and satisfaction which this special achievement has given them, one is reminded of the theme so common to their descriptions of their childhoods. They thought of themselves as "special" children who would "do something." They have "done something," and if they feel a price has been paid, they would still unanimously agree that it was worth it.

In our society, at this place in time, we are finally faced with the recognition that "woman" and "professional" do not really go together yet. A small group of highly gifted and advantaged women have managed to make an amalgamation of the two concepts in their lives, but the union is characterized by continuing tension, both psychic and societal. The women are not liberated, nor are the professional establishments in which they operate. Change will clearly be required of both as society redefines the sex-typing of its vocations.

REFERENCES

Astin, H. S.: *The Woman Doctorate in America.* New York, Russell Sage, 1969.

Bachtold, L. M., and Werner, E. E.: Personality profiles of gifted women: Psychologists. *Am Psychol, 25*:234, 1970.

Baruch, G.: Maternal influences upon college women's attitudes toward women and work. *Developmental Psychology, 6*:32, 1972.

Cartwright, L. K.: Personality and family background of a sample of women medical students at University of California. *J Am Med Wom Assoc, 27* (5) :260, 1972.

Coker, R. E., Back, K. W., Donnelly, T. G., Miller, N., and Phillips, B. S.: Public health as viewed by the medical student. *Am J Public Health, 49* (5):601, 1959.

Epstein, C. F.: Positive effects of the double negative: sex, race, and professional elites. Paper presented at the American Sociological Association Convention, Denver, 1971.

Epstein, C. F.: *Woman's Place.* Berkeley, U Cal Pr, 1971.

Helson, R.: Personalities of women with imaginative and artistic interests: The role of masculinity, originality, and other characteristics of their creativity. *J Pers, 34*:1, 1966.

Hoffman, L. W.: The professional woman as mother. Paper presented at the Conference on Successful Women in the Sciences, New York Academy of Sciences, 1972.

Kaplan, H. I.: Women physicians: The more effective recruitment and utilization of their talents and the resistance to it. *J Am Med Wom Assoc, 25* (9): 561, 1970.

On the job, women act much like men. *Business Week,* October 12, 1963, p. 114.

Psathas, G.: Toward a theory of occupational choice for women. *Sociology and Social Research, 52*:253, 1968.

Rapoport, R., and Rapoport, R. N.: Early and later experiences as determinants of adult behavior. *Br J Sociol, 22*:16, 1971.

Schachter, S.: Birth order, eminence and higher education. *Am Sociol Rev, 28*:757, 1963.

Shapiro, C. S., Stibler, B. J., Zelkovic, A. A., and Mausner, J. S.: Careers of women physicians: A survey of women graduates from seven medical schools, 1945-1951. *J Med Educ, 43:*1033, 1968.

Steinman, A., Levi, J., and Fox, D. J.: Feminine role perceptions of women physicians. *J Am Med Wom Assoc, 17:*776, 1964.

Turner, L., and Turner, B.: Perception of the occupational opportunity structure, socialization to achievement, and career orientation as related to sex and race. Paper presented at the annual meeting of the American Psychological Association, Washington, D. C., 1971.

White, J. J.: Women in the law. *Michigan Law Review, 65:*1051, 1967.

Williams, P. A.: Women in medicine: Some themes and variations. *J Med Educ, 46:*584, 1971.

CHAPTER 2

CAREER ROLES IN MEDICINE

BETTY L. GRUNDY

///

To RELIEVE PAIN and suffering, to stamp out disease, to save lives: to what more laudable goals could one aspire? Ten years out of medical school, fifteen years past my decision on a career in medicine, I find the thrill of successful treatment undiminished. The capable and successful woman in medicine enjoys the respect of her colleagues, the gratitude of her patients, the esteem of the public. She need never doubt the basic worth of her endeavors or her value to society. Intellectual stimulation never lags; constant acquisition of new information is required. Rich interpersonal relationships are developed. A career in medicine, richly rewarding as it may be, is not easily come by. Both training and active practice are intellectually and physically demanding. Hippocrates' statement of twenty-four centuries ago is still applicable.

> Life is short,
> The art long,
> Opportunity fleeting,
> Experience treacherous,
> Judgment difficult.[1]

///

Longevity may have increased, but knowledge has exploded. Long and arduous training is followed by lifelong continuing

---

[1]Hippocrates: Aphorisma Section I, No. 1.

education. The physician who neglects this duty neglects her patients and soon may be unable to practice. Anyone seeking a career in medicine should be inwardly committed to a lifetime of active medical practice and constant education. Personal life-styles must (and certainly can) be developed consistent with these goals. This factor more than any other probably will continue to limit the proportion of doctors who are women. Current trends in our society, though, should open medical careers to more and more capable and dedicated women.

General information on careers in medicine is widely available. Recently, the particular questions concerning women wishing to study and practice medicine have been addressed. It is to these problems we direct our attention. What particular advantages may an increase in the number of women doctors offer our society? What disadvantages? What current trends in medicine and in our society may influence medical careers in the near future, and what particular effects may these changes have on the women physician? Does the aspiring woman physician face discrimination in admission to medical schools, in training, in the practice of medicine? What varieties of medical practice seem most attractive and appropriate for women? What special problems face the doctor who is also wife and mother, and how may these be solved?

Our society seems to have an insatiable demand for physicians' services. Although we are among the richest nations of the world in numbers of doctors, we continually attract foreign-trained physicians to the extent that now one of every six doctors practicing in the United States was trained outside the United States and Canada, and one third of all staff doctors in hospitals with approved internships and residencies are foreign-trained (*U. S. World and News Report,* 1973). Many of these foreign-trained physicians have premedical education inferior to the premedical education of the 13,000 American students turned away from our medical schools each year. Justification of this United States' contribution to the "brain-drain" of many underdeveloped countries, where physicians are scarce, is difficult if not impossible. There are 2,000 Korean doctors presently in the United States, only 13,000 in all of Korea; one sixth of Iran's medical school graduates for the past ten years are currently in this country. There are now more Thai medical school graduates in New York than there are serving the entire rural population (28 million) of Thailand. Increased production of United States' trained physicians is currently under way, with opening of several new medical schools and enlargement of classes in older schools. Capable women may help fill the greater number of available positions in medical schools.

Aside from the increase in total number of physicians, does the woman physician have her own particular contribution to make to society? Probably she does, other factors being equal. Female compassion, gentleness, and tender understanding are invaluable in patient care. Most patients appreciate a little mothering when they are sick or afraid. Also women physicians help to fill a disproportionate number of positions unfilled by men, such as those in clinics, public health and other salaried positions (Bowers, 1966).

Does the woman physician offer society any particular disadvantages as compared to men? There is one, unfortunately. Approximately 9 percent of women fail to practice medicine, compared to less than 1 percent of men (Lopate, 1968). Only 54.5 percent of women physicians graduating between 1931 and 1956 had full-time practices, compared to 88 percent of the men, although 91 percent of the women were practicing either full- or part-time. Furthermore, women physicians often do not work as long hours or attend to as many patients as men, although this may be related primarily to the nature of their practice, (Phelps, 1968) (e.g. salaried positions with fixed hours) or the fact that women physicians generally spend a longer time with each patient than do men. On the average, men in medicine work 30 percent more hours than women and attend one third more patients (Power, Parmlee and Weisenfelder, 1969). Perhaps women may make up some of this deficit in practice hours by greater longevity, but the woman doctor who fails to practice does a grave disservice to her society as well as to other women in medicine.

Women have faced social pressures discouraging aspirations to careers in medicine. These pressures have appropriately eliminated those young women unwilling to make a primary and life-long commitment to a medical career. But perhaps they have needlessly discouraged women who would have made real contributions to society as physicians. As our society becomes more open, allowing men and women alike greater freedom to "do their own thing," and as 43 percent of women enter the labor force, women will have greater opportunities than ever before to pursue demanding careers. At the same time, changing patterns of health care delivery are changing the life-style of all physicians in directions that will make medical careers more and more appealing to intelligent and interested women. Doctors in training are not required to work as long hours as in the past; and with the growth of clinics and group practices, men and women alike are finding more manageable practice hours. These developments should increase the appeal of medical careers to qualified women.

What problems of discrimination may the aspiring woman physician expect to meet? Although real, these are probably less than in many other fields. On the whole, a woman doctor must be a bit more capable than a man to achieve like successes in the practice of medicine. As a doctor friend of my father's told me when I had just decided to apply to medical school: "If you can possible restrain yourself from going into medicine, do. If you can't help yourself, go right ahead. If you're good enough, nobody cares if you're man or woman, black or white."

There is essentially no sex discrimination in acceptance of applicants to medical schools. In 1971, when 12.8 percent of applicants to medical schools were women, 13 percent of students accepted were women. Admission to medical school is based primarily on merit, and since credentials of women applicants were slightly superior to those of men applicants, women were slightly favored for admission (Barclay, 1973).

Once in medical school, women will find judgment again primarily on merit. Though there may be some discrimination against them as women, there will probably be an equal discrimination in their favor. Femininity need not be submerged, but of course, it should not be exploited. If women in medical school accept their position on an equal footing with their male classmates, they will be granted equal status by the men. Women may be subject to some initial "hazing" by men in the classes, as the men seek to determine the social status of these women in the class. If women establish themselves as serious students, friendly, with a sense of humor and a long-term commitment to the practice of medicine, they will quickly gain the respect of their colleagues. If they seek special favors as women or if they become beligerent and aggressive over small or imagined infringements on their equal rights, they may expect the same negative reactions as any other individuals would generate by demanding special favors or being continually abrasive. Certainly, women may enjoy the companionship of their male classmates, although those without outgoing personalities may find that the years in medical school are very lonely.

About 15 percent of women medical students fail to graduate, two thirds of these dropping out during the first year. Over half of these drop outs are in good academic standing and withdraw for personal reasons (Lopate, 1968). Only about 8 percent of male medical students fail to graduate. Medical students have an overall dropout rate of 9 percent compared to 40 percent of all law students, 50 percent of engineering students, and 15 to 20 percent of theological students. Withdrawal of women medical students is apparently unrelated to marital status or family responsibilities and may be due to emotional and social problems engendered by difficulties in role identification for women in a predominantly male group. Few models for role development are available. Perhaps counseling, particularly by successful women physicians, might help lower the dropout rate. Men and women alike may find that maintenance of active interest and friendships outside medicine can add perspective to temporary problems and lend tranquillity to the pace of life.

The variety of medical practice open to the graduating medical student is wider than many realize (Beshiri, 1969). The new woman physician should choose a field compatible with the kind of life-style she wishes to develop. Women who plan to combine the practice of medicine with family responsibilities may wish to choose areas of medicine where practice hours may be definite, with minimal night and weekend work. Positions in research or academic medicine or salaried positions in hospitals or clinics may be convenient. Some may wish to attempt more demanding practices and may be successful in combining these with a satisfactory life at home. Each individual should be realistic in her own decision.

Pediatrics has been the most popular specialty for women, followed by psychiatry, general practice, internal medicine, anesthesiology, obstetrics and gynecology, and pathology (Pennell and Renshaw, 1972). Three fourths of all women physicians practice in these seven areas. Surgical specialties have been more resistant to the acceptance of women, though a few of them would seem to offer ideal practice situations for women. As of 1970, there were only 311 women in this country in general surgery, 307 in ophthalmology, 46 in orthopedic surgery, 52 in otolaryngology, 40 is plastic surgery, and only 36 in the combined fields of neurosurgery, colon and rectal surgery, thoracic surgery, and urology.

Opportunities are greatest and competition least in specialty areas and geographic areas where medical manpower is in short supply. Additionally, women physicians will find their path smoother if they have been preceded by capable women physicians. When I applied for my first job, after a rotating internship, I received a cordial welcome from the personnel director of a mining company. The company had built its own hospital and hired doctors to care for its employees in the nineteenth century as part of a program to recruit miners to the Black Hills of South Dakota. In 1964, the company still hired doctors to care for the miners and their families. The physician-director of the company hospital came over to meet me, and he greeted me thus: "This is a mining town. We're never had a woman doctor here, and we really don't want one. But we're so desperate we have to take anything we can get." The only reasonable response seemed to be a laugh, which emerged spontaneously. The doctor and the personnel director laughed with me, and that was the last I heard of that. I think the doctor was afraid that I wouldn't do a full share of work, wouldn't take my share of night calls and house calls, and wouldn't be accepted by the miners. I was careful to make it clear that my time there would be only about a year—until the end of my husband's tour of duty at a nearby Air Force base—and I think I was able to dispel most of his apprehensions during my year of practice there. I have many fond recollections of that year in general practice. I was warmly received by the community, including the miners. None of the men ever refused any part of a physical examination or treatment. Many of them asked cordially how my husband and I liked the community and whether we might settle there when he left the Air Force. There was one young man who came into my office and asked with a twinkle in his eye whether any of the men ever gave me any trouble; I looked him dead in the eye and said "Not so far." He then went on to tell about his mild case of asthma, which I treated until I left to do my residency in anesthesiology.

Women in private practice today experience minimal overt discrimination. They can compete for patients on the open market. Women who aspire to positions as department heads or to other positions with administrative responsibilities do face definite discrimination at the present time almost universally. Discrimination in group and clinic practice and in salaried positions not involving administrative responsibilities is less but still exists. These latter pockets of discrimination can usually be avoided by those who would rather avoid than fight them. On the whole, the woman physician must still be somewhat more capable and industrious than her male counterpart to achieve the same career goals.

Men and women physicians alike may have trouble reconciling a busy medical career with a satisfactory family life. Women face greater conflicts in this regard because women have traditionally been expected to assume primary responsibility for home and children (*Medical Economics*, 1973). More than three fourths of women physicians are married, over half to other physicians, and most of these have children. Many, but not all, of these doctor mothers work part-time for a few years while children are young. Women who successfully combine medicine and marriage must develop for themselves the most appropriate life-style, and these vary widely. Most married women physicians agree that the biggest factor in successful efforts to combine medicine and marriage is having the right husband. Unless the husband supports the woman doctor's career endeavors, she is usually faced with a choice between divorce and abandoning or seriously curtailing her medical career. Ideally, the woman doctor should marry a man self-confident enough that her professional successes will not threaten his ego.

Most women physicians are unwilling to forego the joys of motherhood, and they often show remarkable ingenuity in developing patterns of living that make motherhood and medical practice quite compatible. Careful planning and wise time utilization are essential. The woman physician may need to build a fairly elaborate supporting network to allow herself time enough for medicine and family. She will be at a great advantage in this endeavor if she delays child-bearing until after the completion of her training.

In conclusion, I would like to describe something of my lifestyle as a woman doctor. At the age of thirty-three, I have a very happy marriage and a wonderful four-year-old daughter who is a source of constant pleasure. I also enjoy a very active and successful medical practice in the field of anesthesiology. I devote more hours per week to medicine than most male physicians, and I devote more hours to my family than many women who are not employed outside the home. How is this possible? First, my husband actively supports my career. He has never objected to the demands of medical training or practice except to question whether I might be overextending myself physically. At the same time, he has always made me feel every inch a woman. Second, I am fortunate enough to be surrounded by capable individuals in every endeavor. My administrative duties as chairman of an anesthesia department in a 330-bed hospital are minimized by a very capable and cooperative Chief Nurse Anesthetist. My efforts in intensive care are maximized by an excellent ICU (intensive care unit) supervisor. A professionally and administratively capable Certified Inhalation Therapy Technician allows the best use of my time as Medical Consultant to the Department of Respiratory Care. Hospital staff work, scheduling of calls and conferences, and general organization of practice responsibilities are managed by an experienced medical secretary who works approximately half-time in my home office. She works primarily from my dictation on cassette tapes kept handy at home and hospital, as well as in my car. In a word, I make every effort to delegate all practice responsibilities that do not require my personal attention and to make as efficient use of my time as possible. To lend proper perspective to this statement, I should add that approximately 50 percent of my time in practice-related activities is nonincome producing.

At home, I depend on a part-time housekeeper who manages cleaning, laundry, and occasional evening baby-sitting. When she is not available, she usually arranges for her mother to help us. During the day, our daughter stays with a family licensed by the state for child care. I began looking for adequate child care early in my pregnancy. My mother stayed with us until our daughter was fourteen months old, when I began taking Jennifer to the family she has spent weekdays with ever since. We wake our daughter early in the morning so that we can enjoy being together before we separate for the day. She takes a long afternoon nap, and we keep her up late in the evening to enjoy another family time together. Essentially all my time is devoted to medicine and my family.

I recognize that I have been more fortunate than many women. In the words of a friend, who happens to be an outstanding musician with a Ph.D. degree, I have "beaten the system." With dedication and careful planning, many intelligent and energetic women can do the same.

I would leave the following final words of advice:

1. Intelligent, energetic, highly motivated women may successfully aspire to richly rewarding medical careers.

2. Women who are unwilling to make a life-long career commitment should not enter medicine.

3. Current trends in our society and in medicine would seem

to offer women physicians greater opportunities than ever before. 4. Marriage and motherhood and medical careers may be successfully combined, although not always easily.

REFERENCES

Barclay, William R.: The future for medical education and women in medicine. *J Am Med Wom Assoc, 28*:69, 1973.

Beshiri, Patricia H.: *The Woman Doctor: Her Career in Modern Medicine.* New York, Cowles, 1969.

Bowers, John Z.: Women in medicine: An international study. *N Engl J Med, 275*:362, 1966.

Lopate, Carol: *Women in Medicine.* Baltimore, Johns Hopkins, 1968. *Medical Economics,* April 30, 1973, p. 191.

Pennell, Maryland Y., and Renshaw, Josephine R.: Distribution of women physicians. *J Am Med Wom Assoc, 27*:197, 1972.

Phelps, Charles E.: Women in American medicine. *J Med Educ, 43*:916, 1968.

Powers, L., Parmlee, R.C., and Wiesenfelder, H.: Practice patterns of women and men physicians. *J Med Educ, 44*:481, 1969.

U.S. News and World Report, July 2, 1973, p. 48.

CHAPTER 3

CAREER ROLES IN DIETETICS

MARGARET BELAIS SALMON

Introduction
Career Opportunities in Dietetics
Education Preparation for the Career of Dietetics
Rewards and Benefits for the Professional Dietician

INTRODUCTION

Dietetics: A Unique Profession

IF YOU ENJOY SERVING mankind and like diversity in your work, a career in dietetics may be the right choice for you. No other profession offers so many opportunities for service in such a wide variety of fields. From coast to coast dietitians are in urgent demand by numerous professions and occupations—communications, medicine, business administration, personnel management, research, architecture, engineering, agriculture, and biochemistry to name just a few. They work part-time or full-time, at home or in an office, in a hospital or laboratory, in schools or on television or radio, or in an industrial setting. And dietetics has the added attraction of being one of the few professions in which you can become more proficient even if you choose to be a full-time homemaker.

What is a dietitian? A dietitian is a man or woman with a college degree who is highly trained in the art and science of feeding human beings, either as individuals or in mass feeding operations. The designation "dietitian" was first applied by the National Home Economics Association in 1899 to the person who specialized in the knowledge of food and who helped to develop diet therapy according to the requirements and standards of the medical profession. Since then the scope of dietetics has broadened, and some of the titles a dietitian may now have are Administrative Dietitian, Air Force Dietitian, Army Dietitian, College or University Teacher, Community Health Consultant, Consultant Educator, Extension Agent, Good Chemist, Food Demonstrator, Food Editor, Food Photographer, Food Researcher, 4-H Club Agent, Hospital Dietitian, Navy Dietitian, Nutritionist, Research Dietitian, Therapeutic Dietitian, and hundreds more. This tremendous variety of opportunities in the field of dietetics has been to me one of its most appealing characteristics. The diversity is not surprising since food supplies a basic human need, and dietitians, through clinical research or the application of improved food information, affect everyone's eating habits, directly or indirectly, from birth to old age.

With the advent of modern food technology dietitians are increasingly in demand. A woman with a bachelor's degree whose major was foods and nutrition, whether she decides to accept a job in the food field or become a full-time homemaker, will still be utilizing her knowledge of dietetics. As a homemaker she can benefit her family with the information she acquired in college about nutrition and food economics. She is in a position to study the latest methods of supermarket merchandising and test new food products, thus increasing her knowledge of contemporary food practices. When she finally returns to a part-time or full-time position she will have become a more valuable employee because of the expertise she gained as a homemaker.

CAREER OPPORTUNITIES IN DIETETICS
Careers in Hospital Dietetics

At present about half of all dietitians are associated with hospitals and/or medical centers. In small hospitals there may be only one dietitian, usually referred to as the *chief dietitian* or *director of dietary services.* She is responsible for all food services in the hospital and plans the budget for the department which might be 10 to 25 percent of the total hospital expenditures. She supervises the purchase and preparation of every food item, arranges the menus, formulates standards for all operations in the dietary department, and develops techniques for training dietary personnel. She also confers with doctors, nurses and patients and teaches diet therapy to medical and nursing students. In a large hospital there may be as many as twenty dietitians or more, each specializing in one area of hospital dietetics—diet therapy, research, administration, teaching or managing food production and food distribution to patients in their individual rooms, or in the special dining rooms (dining rooms for children, psychiatric patients, rehabilitation patients, etc.) and to the hospital staff and visitors.

Teaching hospitals employ dietitians to instruct medical students, nursing students and dietetic interns and to participate in nutrition research. One of the most fascinating positions I've had was as a *research dietitian* in the Department of Pathology at Babies Hospital, Columbia-Presbyterian Medical Center in New York City. As a member of the Cystic Fibrosis Research Team, I instructed patients and their families, calculated their diets, and conferred with doctors on the team. Some of my instruction was conducted by mail, and I corresponded with patients from all over the country.

Hospitals serving patients in outpatient clinics have *clinic dietitians* who instruct patients with specific dietary problems. *Clinic dietitians* either work with groups of patients or on an individual basis. In large clinics a dietitian may counsel hundreds of patients every month. The *clinic dietitian* is mainly interested in diet therapy; she differs from a *therapeutic dietitian* chiefly because the patients she instructs are not hospitalized. In some clinics there may be several *assistant clinic dietitians*. Dietitians who are bilingual are especially in demand in large cities where many different ethnic groups have access to the hospital clinics.

The *therapeutic dietitian* is a specialist with a knowledge of therapeutic nutrition, psychology and dietetics. She cooperates with food service administrators in menu planning and adjusts menu patterns to meet the nutritional needs of those patients for whom a doctor has prescribed a therapeutic diet. She confers with physicians about patients' diets and counsels patients on the planning of diets and menus for use at home and in the hospital. She instructs nursing, dental and medical students and medical and dietetic interns in normal and therapeutic nutrition.

A *teaching dietitian* may be an educational director or a dietetic internship director. She coordinates the nutrition education program within the hospital and teaches nutrition courses. She works with other staff members in planning and organizing the curriculum which is designed to meet the needs of each group of students. The courses may be planned for medical, dental or dietetic interns or patients. She also provides educational programs for the professional staff. *Teaching dietitians* may work full-time or part-time depending on the needs of the hospital. Hospitals affiliated with medical centers provide an extensive educational program which may include instruction in nutrition and diet therapy.

An *administrative dietitian* in a large hospital is a specialist in management and administration. She has administrative assistants who direct the work of food supervisors who are then responsible for food production and distribution. She formulates general departmental policies; employs, trains and supervises personnel; and maintains high standards for food purchasing, production and merchandizing. She maintains cost controls, plans menus, and instructs dietetic interns in basic managerial skills. She develops specifications for dietary equipment and coordinates and evaluates all departmental activities.

Part-time dietitians have opportunities to obtain positions for several hours a week. Some teach in schools of nursing, and many act as *consulting dietitians* in small hospitals, nursing homes, schools, colleges, or state and federal food and nutrition programs and mass feeding operations. *Consulting dietitians* sometimes maintain offices where they confer with clients or patients. *Shared dietitians* are responsible for the dietetic service of small hospitals. They train food service supervisors in hospitals where there are no full-time dietitians and encourage them to maintain high standards of food service.

Dietitians also are employed in several government services. These include the Veterans Administration, Army, Navy, Air Force, and the United States Public Health Service. As medical specialists they are executives who have administrative responsibilities. Professionally qualified dietitians enter this type of service through the United States Civil Service Commission. Also, persons who have a bachelor's degree with a major in foods and nutrition or institution management from an approved college may apply for admission into a dietetic internship which is sponsored by the Veterans Administration and approved by The American Dietetic Association. In the United States Armed Forces, dietitians who hold the rank of commissioned officers may be given assignments in this country or overseas.

The *Army dietitian* is an important member of the medical service team, and works with eminent doctors. The Army dietitian specializes in therapeutics, administration, teaching or research. If a dietitian is accepted into the Army internship he or she is commissioned as a second lieutenant in the Medical Specialist Reserve and is paid on the basis of rank during the year's internship period. The graduate officer then serves as a dietitian for an additional year in an Army hospital. The Army dietitian may then serve for a longer period of active duty as a reserve officer or apply for a regular Army commission and become a military career officer in the Army Medical Specialist Corps.

The *Navy dietitian* serves in Navy hospitals in the United States or outside the country. A person with a bachelor's degree whose major was foods and nutrition or institution management and who is taking a dietetic internship or has been accepted in an internship approved by the American Dietetic Association may receive a Navy commission as an ensign in the Navy's Medical Service Corps. Fully qualified dietitians must agree to serve two or three years from date of appointment. Officers may request for transfer to the regular Navy after completion of eighteen months' active duty. The *Navy dietitian* receives assignments in both the therapeutic and administrative fields, serving in Navy hospitals in the United States or outside the continental limits.

The Air Force Medical Specialist Corps offers a commission as second lieutenant in the Air Force Reserve to qualified degree holders who want to take a civilian dietetic internship approved by The American Dietetic Association. When the internship under this military sponsorship is completed, the graduate is required to serve a two-and one-half-year period on active duty as an *Air Force dietitian*. At the end of the $2\frac{1}{2}$-year period a choice may be made to continue on active duty as a reserve officer or apply for transfer to regular status as an *Air Force Career-officer Dietitian*. The most recent information on careers in the Air Force can be obtained from the headquarters of the United States Air Force at Randolph Air Force Base, Texas.

Dietitians interested in serving in the United States Public Health Service may choose between being a commissioned officer and a Civil Service employee. Commissioned officers in the United States Public Health Service have the salary and rank comparable to those of the other uniformed services and are assigned to one of the United States Public Health hospitals. They specialize in administration, therapeutics, teaching and research. The United States Public Health Service also provides an approved dietetic internship for acceptable candidates who have completed their required college work.

Anyone interested in the careers of dietitians in government services may obtain the most recent and detailed information by writing directly to the service in question. Write to the Public Health Service, Department of Health, Education and Welfare or the Department of the Army or Navy in Washington, D.C.

The *S. S. Hope,* a floating hospital, provides an opportunity to travel for dietitians who enjoy serving a variety of ethnic groups. Dietitians on the *S. S. Hope* work with nursing and medical staff on the ship and teach diet therapy to patients and dietary personnel in other countries. They must have a minimum of two years hospital experience, have language aptitude, and teaching and supervisory experience.

Careers of Dietitians in Business

Dietitians who enjoy "meeting the public" or have talent for writing, editing, promotion and speaking may find their niche in industry or business. Some of the most extraordinary experiences I've had as a dietitian have been working with food companies and newspaper editors either as a foods and nutrition consultant or in connection with recipe development and recipe judging. One assignment was as a recipe judge for a large suburban newspaper. For eight years the newspaper sponsored an annual contest, and each time over two thousand readers submitted their favorite recipes. Eager contestants spelled out every detail from the exact location in the Hackensack River to catch turtles for fresh turtle soup to the number of minutes you could bathe your baby while lemon pudding gelled to the consistency of a raw egg white. One hundred and forty of the best recipes were arranged into a cookbook after each contest, and judges taste-tested every recipe in the book—one hundred and forty different gourmet dishes all taste-tested in one day!

Food equipment and utility companies and trade associations hire dietitians to conduct their programs in nutrition research, education and promotion. Experienced dietitians direct these activities and are assisted by other food experts (home economists, food chemists and assistant dietitians). Some of their duties include research to determine the nutritional value of food products, chemical analysis of foods (vitamin and mineral research), originating and standardizing recipes for publication, writing research papers, and developing recipe books.

Large food companies recruit dietitians to run experimental test kitchens where the firm's products are developed into menu items. These dietitians may participate in radio and television programs in connection with their company's products. They help with advertising copy, and they write instructions on the use of the company's products. Dietitians experienced in food photography also work with magazine editors and television directors in connection with promotion for food companies.

Dietitians working for food equipment and utility companies; advertising agencies; and manufacturing, processing and distributing firms serve largely in promotional activities. Their knowledge of the chemistry of foods as well as their training in psychology, communications, nutrition, and related fields make them valuable assets to their employers. For example, in utility companies they organize consumer programs for the purpose of demonstrating to housewives the correct use of electrical kitchen appliances. They conduct classes on food preparation, preservation and refrigeration, and write informative booklets for consumers.

Careers of Dietitians in Research

Research in foods and nutrition is especially attractive to dietitians with a strong background in chemistry. *Research dietitians* usually have advanced academic degrees with special emphasis on the sciences. They find positions in nutrition research laboratories of medical centers, colleges, universities, business organizations, and governmental agencies. They conduct experiments on food preservation and develop improved techniques for measuring the quality, flavor and nutritive values of foods. In colleges, universities, and medical centers dietitians work with professors of pathology, microbiology, biochemistry, and foods and nutrition who are responsible for much of the progress in dietetics.

Dietitians' education in the behaviorial sciences prepare them for research on factors affecting food habits and dietary patterns. They participate in community research projects in an attempt to develop new and improved public health programs. These projects are supported by federal agencies, state and local health departments, universities, medical centers, and grants from industry. The studies may be carried out with individuals in their own homes, at their place of employment, in hospitals, and in extended care facilities. An example might be a study by a dietitian working with pregnant women who attend a hospital clinic. One group of women receives a special high-potency nutrition supplement during pregnancy, and the dietitian calculates the dietary intake of both groups, one group acting as a control. Finally, the condition of the newborn infants of both groups of women is carefully compared. A nutritionist or dietitian in such a study would be working with a team of professional researchers including physicians, nurses, biostatisticians, biochemists, psychologists, social scientists, and others.

Careers of Dietitians in Commercial and Industrial Food Service

Dietitians with administrative ability have opportunities to direct mass feeding operations in restaurants, tearooms, hotel dining rooms, coffee shops, department store restaurants, and industrial cafeterias. An administrative dietitian in commercial food service and industry has all of the duties of an administrative hospital dietitian plus the additional challenge of developing the ability to make a profit for her employer. She must have a sense of showmanship in her arrangement of attractive food displays and innovative ideas for encouraging patrons to select her particular food operation.

In industrial in-plant food service facilities the dietitian has an opportunity to encourage workers to increase their productivity by teaching them to make nutritious food selections. In some industrial organizations dietitians serve as nutrition advisors, and in others they may work with the medical department as a dietary consultant to employees.

Careers of Dietitians in the Community

Dietitians who like to work with people and are especially interested in the science of nutrition work as community nutritionists. They must have an advanced degree in nutrition education, public health nutrition, or the science of nutrition. Nutritionists who serve the community aim to help others live healthier lives. They learn to interpret the science of nutrition into clear and logical instructions that the public can understand and follow. Nutritionists have titles such as *County Nutritionist, State Nutritionist* or *Public Health Nutritionist*. They may conduct nutrition programs for a visiting nurse association, a public or privately endowed voluntary organization such as The American Red Cross, The American Heart Association, or a public health agency. Through teaching, writing and consultation nutritionists reach directly or indirectly many families who profit by their advice in buying, preparing and serving food for the nutritional needs of each member of the family group.

A nutritionist with the extension service of a state college or university is called an *Extension Service Nutritionist.* She works in small communities where she teaches people to adapt available foods to their own eating patterns. She instructs people with limited incomes about food values and the importance of good nutrition for every member of the family.

A nutritionist who works for a city, county, state or federal public health program is called a *Public Health Nutritionist.* She teaches nutrition to large groups of people, both professional and nonprofessional. She also prepares pamphlets, exhibits and films and gives talks on radio and television.

Careers of Teaching Dietitians

In every phase of dietetics occasions arise when dietitians assume the role of teachers. It may be teaching nutrition to medical students in a hospital or food sanitation to dietary employees, but it usually is just one facet of the dietitian's daily agenda. However, dietitians who spend the majority of their time as instructors are called *teaching dietitians.* They may teach foods and nutrition in a school of nursing or courses in a dietetic internship program. Dietitians with advanced degrees teach a variety of subjects in colleges and universities. They instruct students in diet therapy, normal human nutrition, advanced nutrition, food research, food chemistry, human metabolism, institution management, accounting, economics, contemporary food practices, modern food technology, techniques of space feeding, and many others. The list of subjects expands continuously as modern research opens up unexplored vistas in the world of food.

EDUCATIONAL PREPARATION FOR THE CAREER OF DIETETICS

In high school a college preparatory course with an emphasis on science is the first step to take toward a career in dietetics. Courses such as biology, chemistry and physics will help you decide whether you have an interest in the sciences and prepare you for college science courses required for a degree in foods and nutrition. Your guidance counselor can help you select accredited colleges offering degrees in foods and nutrition (see Table 3-III at end of chapter). Experience you obtain as a volunteer or part-time worker in a local hospital dietary department might help you decide if you would enjoy being a hospital dietitian.

After acceptance into an accredited college you can arrange a four-year program leading to a bachelor's degree in foods and nutrition or institution management. Required courses include human physiology, microbiology, inorganic and organic chemistry, biochemistry, personnel management, economics, accounting, sociology, psychology, physiology, human nutrition, creative or technical writing, and learning theory or educational methods (see requirements at end of chapter).

On completion of the Bachelor of Science degree you are qualified to apply for admission to a dietetic internship program. These programs are usually under the direction of registered dietitians. There are a variety of dietetic internship programs approved by the American Dietetic Association. Some stress normal nutrition and diet therapy, some emphasize general hospital dietetics, and some concentrate on food service administration. The internships last approximately one year, although recently, due to the increased demand for dietitians, some of these programs have been concentrated into periods shorter than twelve months. During the internship you have an opportunity to put into practice knowledge you acquired in college. You attend classes and learn, under the guidance of foods and nutrition specialists, the responsibilities of a professional dietitian. Then after satisfactory completion of graduate education as a dietetic intern in a program approved by the American Dietetic Association, a dietitian is eligible for membership in the ADA, the national organization of the profession of dietetics. Membership in the American Dietetic Association distinguishes professionally qualified dietitians from those in the food field with less extensive preparation.

The American Dietetic Association was founded in 1917 by a

small group of dietitians who wanted to help the country's war-time food conservation program. The objectives of the American Dietetic Association are to improve the nutrition of human beings, to advance the science of dietetics and nutrition, and to promote education in these and allied areas. In 1969 voluntary registration was established to encourage high standards of performance by members of the American Dietetic Association. Members of the American Dietetic Association who wish to become registered dietitians (R.D.) must successfully pass a comprehensive examination on nutrition and dietetics and continue their education on the graduate level in special advanced educational programs.

In 1971 there were approximately eighty approved dietetic internship programs in hospitals and other institutions throughout the United States. A year later in 1972, although over 1800 students applied to these programs, only 850 could be accepted due to lack of facilities even though many were well qualified! To alleviate this situation some experienced members of the American Dietetic Association have organized dietetic traineeship-preplanned programs (approved by the American Dietetic Association) for dietitians who want to work full-time while they accumulate enough experience to become members of the American Dietetic Association. These preplanned programs usually take from one to two years to complete.

At St. Joseph's Hospital and Medical Center in Paterson, New Jersey, we have three dietitians in preplanned programs, two with bachelor's degrees in foods and nutrition and one with a master's degree. There must be at least two experienced staff dietitians (each of whom is a member of the American Dietetic Association and preferably registered) participating in a dietetic traineeship-preplanned program. And in each program there must be one or more experienced ADA staff dietitians than there are trainees, i.e. two dietitians for one trainee, three dietitians for two trainees. Lists of current approved dietetic internship programs and dietetic traineeship-preplanned programs may be obtained from the American Dietetic Association, 620 North Michigan Avenue, Chicago, Illinois, 60611.

Financing Your Educational Preparation for a
Career in Dietetics

On July 2, 1862, President Abraham Lincoln signed the Morrill Land-Grant College Act which authorized giving to each state free public land that the state could sell or use for the creation or development of institutions of higher learning. A goal of the Morrill Act was "to have at least one institution of higher learning in every state, accessible to all." There are seventy land-grant colleges and universities graduating men and women who go on to hundreds of different types of jobs in the food field. These institutions offer not only subjects specifically about foods and nutrition but also courses in microbiology, biochemistry, business administration and many others. Some land-grant colleges even have schools of public health, and all of them give students the opportunity to attend college with minimum expenditures.

Information about the location of land-grant colleges and universities can be obtained from the United States Department of Agriculutre. Your guidance counselor can give you additional information on foods and nutrition courses offered in private colleges. Before making a decision it would be wise to check with the American Dietetic Association to make certain that the undergraduate program you select offers all the courses that are necessary prerequisites for an ADA approved dietetic internship program.

The American Dietetic Association and The American Dietetic Association Foundation offer financial aid to dietetic interns and undergraduate and graduate students. The American Dietetic Association Foundation was organized in 1966 by the American Dietetic Association and administers twenty undergraduate scholarships and five graduate scholarships. The American Dietetic Association offers loans to members who are graduate students and dietetic interns as well as scholarships donated by members of the American Dietetic Association (see list at end of chapter).

Many dietetic internship programs provide room, board and professional laundry service and almost all pay a stipend to the dietetic intern. Some internships are affiliated with a college or university so that you can accumulate graduate credits while taking your dietetic internship. During my own dietetic internship at Duke University Hospital in North Carolina, I earned graduate credits at Duke University and had a part-time job as an assistant to the head of the Biochemistry Department. In the Biochemistry Department we studied the effects of B vitamin deficiencies resulting from the vitamin poor diets patients were eating—mainly hominy grits, fat back and corn bread. Seeing that patients with pellagra who had the typical symptoms of dermatitis, diarrhea and dementia could be cured by good nutrition was a lesson I never forgot.

Earning while you learn is another way to finance your education in dietetics. Drexel University in Philadelphia is one of the pioneers in work-study programs for college students. At Drexel University men and women may accumulate as much as two years of practical experience, and at the same time earn a bachelor's degree in a college program specifically preplanned for each individual student. The college arranges for the student to work in a pertinent industry, and the employer then reports to the college on the student's performance and pays the student a prearranged salary.

Many hospitals and institutions employ college students in their dietary departments. Some students earn enough during vacation periods and free days to pay for their college tuition, and foods and nutrition students gain valuable experience by working in food service operations. At St. Joseph's Hospital several college students assist us in our dietary department, and their school grades are better than average because they are "learning by doing" in real life situations, not solely from their textbooks. We find that college students are an asset to our department in many ways, and their energy and enthusiasm boost the morale of the other employees.

REWARDS AND BENEFITS FOR THE PROFESSIONAL DIETITIAN

What are the rewards and benefits a professional dietitian can expect? In the profession of dietetics salaries vary considerably and depend on experience, number of advanced degrees received, willingness to accept responsibility, location of the position, and the supply of dietitians available. In general, salaries are as good or better than those with comparable professional training. Recently salaries have risen as the complexity and scope of dietetics has increased. It is not uncommon for dietitians in large institutions to be responsible for the production of thousands of meals a day. Naturally, high salaries would be paid to dietitians in this type of position. Only a skilled dietitian with enthusiasm, good health, experience, creativity, and ability to motivate employees could cope with such a challenge. Dietitians with less demanding positions would receive salaries commensurate with their responsibilities.

In conclusion, dietitians are trained to be leaders and teachers; work with all types of people, professional and nonprofessional; and maintain high standards of personal health and emotional maturity. At the present time most dietitians are women, but the number of male dietitians is increasing steadily. As mentioned above, salaries vary considerably, but *all* dietitians receive the rich reward that comes when you know you are filling a need and helping people to attain happier, healthier lives. Dietetics is a career that challenges you mentally and physically, a career in which you are judged by your achievements and not your race, creed, or ethnic background, and a career that gives you the satisfaction of knowing you have helped anywhere from one to hundreds of people every working day. If these are the rewards you are seeking, then you'll enjoy a career in dietetics.

TABLE 3-I.
THE AMERICAN DIETETIC ASSOCIATION
620 North Michigan Avenue, Chicago, Ill. 60611
MINIMUM ACADEMIC REQUIREMENTS — PLAN IV
BASIC REQUIREMENTS PLUS ONE AREA OF SPECIALIZATION*

AREA OF SUBJECT MATTER	BASIC REQUIREMENTS	AREAS OF SPECIALIZATION IN DIETETICS			
		General	Management	Clinical	Community
Physical & Biological Sciences	Chemistry, inorganic and organic Human physiology Microbiology	Biochemistry		Biochemistry Biochemical analysis [b]Anatomy or [b]advanced physiology or [b]genetics	Biochemistry
Behavioral & Social Sciences	Sociology or psychology (principles) Economics	Cultural anthropology or sociology	Labor economics or relations	Cultural anthropology or sociology	Cultural anthropology or sociology [c]Psychology
Professional Sciences	Food (composition, physical and chemical changes, quality, acceptability, and aesthetics) Prerequisite: organic chemistry Nutrition Prerequisites: human physiology & organic chemistry Management theory and principles	Food service systems management Nutrition in disease Prerequisite: biochemistry	Food service systems management Principles of business organization (Management of personnel Financial management	Additional nutrition course Prerequisite: biochemistry Nutrition in disease Prerequisite: biochemistry	Nutrition in disease Prerequisite: biochemistry Nutrition and community health Prerequisite: biochemistry Food service systems management (volume food service in the community)

| Communication Sciences | Writing (creative or technical)
 ªMathematics (competency equal to intermediate algebra)
 Learning theory or educational methods | ᵇData processing (computer logic) or ᵇData evaluation (statistics) | Data processing (computer logic) or Data evaluation (statistics) | Data evaluation (statistics) | Data evaluation (statistics) |

ªMay be acquired prior to college entrance.

ᵇRecommended, not required

ᶜIf not completed in basic requirements

*Minimum Academic Requirements are expressed in terms of *basic competencies* rather than in specific credit hours, in *knowledge areas*, not in courses.

The College or University's plan for meeting these academic requirements must be approved by the ADA before they can be applied to the individual student.

TABLE 3-II.

THE AMERICAN DIETETIC ASSOCIATION

620 North Michigan Avenue

Chicago, Illinois   60611

SOURCES FOR UNDERGRADUATE AND DIETETIC INTERNSHIP
SCHOLARSHIPS

THE AMERICAN DIETETIC ASSOCIATION — administers scholarships to undergraduate college students entering junior and senior years and to college students accepted for an approved dietetic internship.

STATE DIETETIC ASSOCIATIONS — usually give scholarships to the senior student in college or the college student accepted for an approved dietetic internship.
(Write ADA for contact in each state.)

THE AMERICAN HOME ECONOMICS ASSOCIATION (2010 Massachusetts Avenue, N.W., Washington, D.C.   20036) — has information on financial aid to undergraduate students in home economics.

THE AMERICAN LEGION EDUCATION & SCHOLARSHIP PROGRAM (De-
partment S, P. O. Box 1055, Indianapolis, IN   46206) — annually revises and pub-
lishes NEED A LIFT, a handbook with sources for scholarships and details on
selected ones. Price 25c or 5 for $1.00.

ARMY MEDICAL SPECIALISTS CORPS (The Surgeon General, Department of
the Army, Washington, D.C.   20315) — sponsors the program, "Student Dietitian"
for college students at the junior or senior level. (It requires a certain period of
service in the Army.)

NATIONAL RESTAURANT ASSOCIATION (1530 N. Lake Shore Dr., Chicago,
IL   60611) — administers Heinz scholarships to students interested in food careers.
*Consult PUBLIC LIBRARY for one of the following publications on scholarship
opportunities:*

These books are updated regularly. Ask your librarian for the most recent editions.
Also, please note that some reference volumes include home economics opportunities under Liberal Arts entries.

Fellowships in Arts and Sciences. Published by the American Council on Education,
   1 Dupont Circle, Washington, D.C.   20036.

Graduate Study in the United States. A guide for foreign students who plan to do
   graduate study in the United States. Prepared in cooperation with the Council
   of Graduate Schools. Institute of International Education, 809 United Nations
   Plaza, New York, NY   10017.

Grants for Graduate Study Abroad. Graduate-study awards under the Fulbright-
   Hays Act and fellowships for U.S. students to study abroad offered by foreign
   governments, universities, and private donors. Institute of International Education, 809 United Nations Plaza, New York, NY   10017.

Lovejoy Scholarship Guide. Published by Simon and Schuster, Inc., New York.

National Register of Scholarships and Fellowships. Volume 1, "Scholarships and Loans"; Volume 2, "Fellowships and Grants." By Juvenal Angel. World Trade Academy Press, New York.

Scholarships, Fellowships and Loans. By Norman Feingold. Published by Bellman Publishing Company, Cambridge, MA. Three volumes.

NOTE: Many colleges, universities, and other educational institutions have a scholarship fund, loan fund, or other service such as a student employment office. If you have already been accepted at a university, ask about possible financial aids.

Home economics departments may have assistantships, scholarships, and fellowships available to undergraduate students. Interested students should write directly to the head of the home economics department of the college or university of his choice for information.

Other sources of scholarships include: the federal and state government; private organizations, such as alumni groups, business and industry; and civic organizations.

TABLE 3-III.

THE AMERICAN DIETETIC ASSOCIATION
620 North Michigan Avenue
Chicago, Illinois 60611

COLLEGES AND UNIVERSITIES OFFERING A BACCALAUREATE DEGREE
WITH A MAJOR IN DIETETICS

There are other institutions offering a major in dietetics. If you are interested in attending a college or university not listed here, it is suggested you write the school to learn (1) if it is approved by a Regional Accrediting Agency of Higher Education, and (2) if it offers the courses needed to meet academic requirements for membership in The American Dietetic Association.

ALABAMA
Alabama Agricultural and Mechanical
University, Normal 35762
Auburn University, Auburn 36830
Tuskegee Institute, Tuskegee Institute 36088
University of Alabama, University 35486

ARIZONA
Arizona State University, Tempe 85281
Northern Arizona Univ., Flagstaff 86001
University of Arizona, Tucson 85721

ARKANSAS
Arkansas AM&N College, Pine Bluff 71601
Harding College, Searcy 72143
Philander Smith College, Little Rock 72203
Univ. of Arkansas, Fayetteville 72701

CALIFORNIA
Calif. State College at Long Beach 90801
Calif. State College at Los Angeles 90032
Calif. State Poly. College, Pomona 91766
Calif. State Poly. College,
   San Luis Obispo 93401
Chico State College, Chico 95926
College of Notre Dame, Belmont 94002
Fresno State College, Fresno 93726
Immaculate Heart College, Los Angeles 90027
Loma Linda Univ., La Sierra Campus
   Riverside 92505
Pacific Union College, Angwin 94508
San Diego State College, San Diego 92115
San Fernando Valley State College,
   Northridge 91324

San Jose State College, San Jose 95114
Univ. of Calif., Berkeley 94720
Univ. of Calif., Davis 95616
Univ. of Calif., Los Angeles 90024
Univ. of Calif., Santa Barbara 93106
Whittier College, Whittier 90605
San Francisco State College,
   San Francisco 94132

COLORADO
Colorado State Univ., Ft. Collins 80521
University of Northern Colorado, Greeley 80631

CONNECTICUT
St. Joseph College, W. Hartford 06117
University of Conn., Storrs 06268

DELAWARE
University of Delaware, Newark 19711

DISTRICT OF COLUMBIA
Howard University, Washington 20001

FLORIDA
Barry College, Miami 33161
Florida A&M University, Tallahassee 32307
Florida State Univ., Tallahassee 32306

GEORGIA
Clark College, Atlanta 30314
Berry College, Mount Berry 30149
Fort Valley State College, Fort Valley 31030
Savannah State College, Savannah 31404
University of Georgia, Athens 30601
Georgia College at Milledgeville, 31061

HAWAII
University of Hawaii, Honolulu 96822

IDAHO
University of Idaho, Moscow 83843

ILLINOIS
Barat College of the Sacred Heart,
   Lake Forest 60045
Eastern Ill. Univ., Charleston 61920
Illinois Wesleyan Univ., Bloomington 61701
Mundelein College, Chicago 60626

Northern Illinois Univ., DeKalb 60115
Olivet Nazarene College, Kankakee 60901
Rosary College, River Forest 60305
Southern Illinois Univ., Carbondale 62901
University of Illinois, Urbana 61801

INDIANA
Ball State University, Muncie 47306
Goshen College, Goshen 46526
Indiana State Univ., Terre Haute 47809
Indiana University, Bloomington 47401
Manchester College, North Manchester 46962
Marian College, Indianapolis 46222
Purdue University, Lafayette 47907
St. Marys-of-the-Woods College,
   St. Mary-of-the-Woods 47876
Valparaiso University, Valparaiso 46383

IOWA
Clarke College, Dubuque 52001
Iowa State University, Ames 50010
Iowa Wesleyan College, Mt. Pleasant 52641
Marycrest College, Davenport 52804
University of Iowa, Iowa City 52240

KANSAS
Kansas State Teachers College, Emporia 66801
Kansas State University, Manhattan 66502
Mt. St. Scholastic College, Atchison 66002
St. Benedict's College, Atchison 66002
St. Mary College, Xavier 66098

KENTUCKY
Berea College, Berea 40403
Catherine Spalding College, Louisville 40203
Eastern Kentucky Univ., Richmond 40475
Morehead State University, Morehead 40351
University of Kentucky, Lexington 40506
Western Kentucky Univ., Bowling Green 42101

LOUISIANA
Grambling College, Grambling 71245
Louisiana Tech., Ruston 71270
Louisiana State Univ., Baton Rouge 70803
Northwestern St. Col., Natchitoches 71457
St. Mary's Dominican College,
   New Orleans 70118
Southeastern Louisiana Col., Hammond 70401

Southern University, Baton Rouge 70813
Univ. of Southwestern Louisiana,
    Lafayette 70501

MAINE
University of Maine, Orono 04473

MARYLAND
Columbia Union College, Takoma Park 20012
Hood College, Frederick 21701
Maryland State College, Princess Anne 21853
Morgan State College, Baltimore 21212
St. Joseph College, Emmitsburg 21727
Univ. of Maryland, College Park 20740

MASSACHUSETTS
Atlantic Union College, So. Lancaster 01561
Simmons College, Boston 02115
State College at Framingham 01701
Univ. of Massachusetts, Amherst 01002

MICHIGAN
Eastern Mich. University, Ypsilanti 48197
Andrews University, Berrien Springs 49104
Marygrove College, Detroit 48221
Mercy College of Detroit, Detroit 48219
Michigan State Univ., E. Lansing 48823
Northern Michigan Univ., Marquette 49855
Wayne State University, Detroit 48202
Western Michigan Univ., Kalamazoo 49001

MINNESOTA
The College of St. Catherine, St. Paul 55116
College of St. Scholastica, Duluth 55811
College of St. Teresa, Winona 55987
Mankato State College, Mankato 56001
Univ. of Minnesota, St. Paul 55101

MISSISSIPPI
Miss. State College for Women, Columbus 39701
Mississippi State Univ., State College 39762
Univ. of Southern Miss., Hattiesburg 39401
The Univ. of Miss., University 38677

MISSOURI
Central Missouri State College,
    Warrensburg 64093
Drury College, Springfield 65802
Fontbonne College, St. Louis 63105
Lincoln Univ., Jefferson City 65101

Southwest Missouri St. Col., Springfield 65802
University of Missouri, Columbia 65201

MONTANA
Montana State University, Bozeman 59715
University of Montana, Missoula 59801

NEBRASKA
Kearney State College, Kearney 68847
Union College, Lincoln 68506
University of Nebraska, Lincoln 68503
University of Nebraska, Omaha 68101

NEVADA
University of Nevada, Reno 89502

NEW HAMPSHIRE
Mt. St. Mary College, Hocksett 03106
Rivier College, Nashua 03060
University of New Hampshire, Durham 03824

NEW JERSEY
College of St. Elizabeth, Convent Station 07961
Douglass College, New Brunswick 08903
Montclair State College, Montclair 07043

NEW MEXICO
New Mexico State Univ., Las Cruces 88001
Univ. of New Mexico, Albuquerque 87106

NEW YORK
Cornell University, Ithaca 14850
Herbert H. Lehman College, Cuny, N. Y. 10001
Hunter College CUNY, N. Y. 10021
Marymount College, Tarrytown 10591
New York Univ., New York City 10003
Pratt Institute, Brooklyn 11205
Rochester Institute of Technology 14623
State Univ. College, Buffalo 14222
State Univ. College, Oneonta 13820
State Univ. College, Plattsburgh 12901
State Univ. of New York, Brooklyn 11203
Syracuse University, Syracuse 13210
Queens College, CUNY, Flushing 11367

NORTH CAROLINA
Appalachian State Univ., Boone 28608
East Carolina Univ., Greenville 27834
North Carolina A&T St. Univ.,
    Greensboro 27411

TABLE 3-III.—(Continued)

North Carolina Central U., Durham 27707
North Carolina College, Durham 27707
Univ. of North Carolina, Greensboro 27412

NORTH DAKOTA
North Dakota State Univ., Fargo 58102
Univ. of North Dakota, Grand Forks 58201

OHIO
Baldwin-Wallace College, Berea 44017
Bowling Green Univ., Bowling Green 43402
Case Western Reserve Univ., Cleveland 44106
Central State College, Wilburforce 45384
College of Mt. St. Joseph-on-the-Ohio,
  Mt. St. Joseph 45051
Edgecliff College, Cincinnati 45238
Kent State University, Kent 44240
Miami University, Oxford 45056
Notre Dame College, Cleveland 44121
Ohio Dominican College, Columbus 43219
Ohio University, Athens 45701
Ohio Wesleyan Univ., Delaware 43015
Our Lady of Cincinnati College,
  Cincinnati 45206
The Ohio State Univ., Columbus 43210
University of Akron, Akron 44304
University of Cincinnati, 45221
University of Dayton, Dayton 45409
Ursuline College, Cleveland 44124
Western College for Women, Oxford 45056
Youngstown Univ., Youngstown 44503

OKLAHOMA
Oklahoma State University, Stillwater 74074
University of Oklahoma, Norman 73069

OREGON
Oregon State University, Corvallis 97331

PENNSYLVANIA
College Misericordia, Dallas 18612
Drexel Institute of Technology,
  Philadelphia 19104
Immaculata College, Immaculata 19345
Indiana Univ. of Penn., Indiana 15701
Mansfield State College, Mansfield 16933
Marywood College, Scranton 18509
Pennsylvania State Univ.,
  University Park 16802

Seton Hill College, Greensburg 15601
Villa Maria College, Erie 16506

PUERTO RICO
Univ. of Puerto Rico, Rio Piedras 00931

RHODE ISLAND
Univ. of Rhode Island, Kingston 02881

SOUTH CAROLINA
South Carolina State College,
  Orangeburg 29115

SOUTH DAKOTA
South Dakota State Univ., Brookings 57006

TENNESSEE
David Lipscomb College, Nashville 37203
Memphis State Univ., Memphis 38111
Middle Tenn. State Univ., Murfreesboro 37130
Southern Missionary College,
  Collegedale 37315
Tennessee A&T State Univ., Nashville 37203
Tenn. Technological Univ., Cookeville 38501
The Univ. of Tennessee, Knoxville 37916
Belmont College, Nashville 37203

TEXAS
Incarnate Word College, San Antonio 78209
North Texas State Univ., Denton 76203
Our Lady of the Lake College,
  San Antonio 78207
Prairie View A&M College, Prairie View 77445
Southwestern Union College, Keene 76059
Texas A&T State Univ., Kingsville 78203
Texas Christian Univ., Ft. Worth 76129
Texas Southern University, Houston 77004
Texas Tech. College, Lubbock 79409
Texas Woman's University, Denton 76204
University of Houston, Houston 77004
The University of Texas, Austin 78712
The University of Texas, Dallas 75061

UTAH
Brigham Young University, Provo 84601
Univ. of Utah, Salt Lake City 84112
Utah State University, Logan 84321

TABLE 3-III.—(Continued)

ERMONT
niversity of Vermont, Burlington 05401

IRGINIA
astern Mennonite College, Harrisonburg 22801
ampton Institute, Hampton 23368
ladison College, Harrisonburg 22801
lary Washington College of the Univ. of
 Virginia, Fredericksburg 22401
adford College, Radford 24141
irginia Polytechnic Institute, Blacksburg 24061
irginia State College, Petersburg 23806

ASHINGTON
astern Wa. State College, Cheney 99004
rt Wright College of the Holy Names,
 Spokane 99204
niv. of Washington, Seattle 98105
alla Walla College, College Place 99324

Washington State Univ., Pullman 99163

WEST VIRGINIA
Marshall University, Huntington 25701
West Va. State College, Institute 25112
W. Virginia Univ., Morgantown 26506
W. Virginia Wesleyan College,
 Buckhannon 26201

WISCONSIN
Cardinal Stritch College, Milwaukee 53217
Mount Mary College, Milwaukee 53222
Stout State Univ., Menomonie 54751
Univ. of Wisconsin, Madison 53706
Viterbo College, La Crosse 54601
Wis. State Univ., Stevens Point 55481

WYOMING
Univ. of Wyoming, Laramie 82070

CHAPTER 4

THE WOMAN
IN THE BUSINESS OF ECONOMICS

VIRGINIA LEE McKEMIE-BELT

What or Who Is an Economist?
The Business Environment
Economic Education
Career Opportunities in "Pure" Economics
Applied Economics—A Bagful of Career Opportunities
Conclusion

YOUNG BUSINESSWOMEN are fortunate persons today. They are accepted as essential workers in our free enterprise system. A young woman who majors in economics or business can find many areas where she can bring special talents to the job. She can succeed because she can offer different viewpoints and different innate abilities from men.

The young businesswoman today does not need to be a feminist. She should not go into the business world with a chip on her shoulder and with the idea that to succeed she has to militantly compete with men. She only needs to do her job a little better. In many industries today where governmental agencies are pressuring companies to increase their hiring of minorities and women, she may get a job "in spite of her qualifications" and solely because of her sex. The young woman should remember, though, that if she's hired solely to meet some exogenous requirements she won't "go

50

anywhere" with the firm unless she can demonstrate unusual abilities. Take advantage of the fact that being a woman opened the doors, but then exert every effort to prove that you should have been hired because of your abilities and your suitableness for the job.

As a professional competing in a male-dominated field (finance), I've found some doors closed too tightly to open—like the large university that cancelled an employment interview for which they had already advanced traveling money when they learned that V. Mc-Kemie-Belt, Ph.D., was a young woman. I have had some interesting experiences—like the time I arranged to have a university stock market class of forty-nine males visit an exchange. The public relations firm for the exchange decided to use the class visit for some publicity shots and releases. Because women were not allowed on the floor of the exchange, I sat with an apologetic V.P. in the Board Room while my students got a rare and rewarding look at the floor operations. Or like the time I was invited along with twenty-nine male colleagues from across the nation to join a similar group of "men from Wall Street" to discuss university/investment community joint actions. I was selected by the faculty representatives to address about 300 members of the investment community and outline our responses to the various plans of actions that had been proposed. When we arrived at the very prestigious Exchange Club, I was barred from entry because of my sex. When the officials of the club learned that I was the guest speaker, they arranged for me to be admitted to this all-male bastion by way of the freight elevator and kitchen. Or like the time I was scheduled to address the representative of the investment and banking community in Singapore. After dinner and introductions, I stood and all the Oriental gentlemen in the audience stood also. I immediately sat down; so did they. Then I stood again and to my consternation, the audience stood again. Finally the host convinced them that I would consider it no disrespect if they sat while I, a woman, stood. However, for the most part, I have experienced no discrimination and have had an equal opportunity to succeed. The young woman entering the business world as an economist should find it even easier today.

Can the young woman economist successfully combine a career

and marriage? There is nothing inherent in the business of being an economist that would make that field less amenable to a career/ marriage combination than in any other field. However, as is so often the case, the young businesswoman finds herself so involved in her business that an average day is likely to become ten to twelve or more hours. Therefore, her time with the family is severely restricted. The challenge and excitement of succeeding in a business career is often such that even her hours at home are devoted in time and thought to tomorrow's deal or client or decision. She must honestly ask herself whether the husband/wife relationship can stand these hours and concentration. The woman economist should be more aware than most married working women whether her job actually contributes to the economic well-being of the family. All of the intrinsic costs (missing food and product sales, convenience buying, speedy decisions) as well as the explicit costs (new clothes, hair do's, extra taxes, carfare, hired help) must be carefully computed. Often, too, a young woman in business is promoted rapidly or her business venture succeeds beyond her wildest dreams or she outsells her male competitors. She must be aware that, while her increased income is welcome, her husband's ego is easily bruised. She must walk a tightrope between her husband's pride and his natural resentment. Often her income exceeds his, and if she values her marriage, that fact must be forgotten in conversation with him and with others. Many a woman has considered her income as hers, bankable, and extra and her husband's income as family income out of which all family bills and expenses should come. This is not true. She owes the family for time and effort which she cannot devote to it, so her income is also family income.

Finally, marriage can bring to the businesswoman a greater understanding of the needs and wants of her clients. Social adjustment, financial acumen, and real womanliness *are* expected of the businesswoman who uses her experience and abilities to combine business life and home life. It is not an easy task, but it is challenging and productive of self-satisfying accomplishments. *And* it can be done. Next month, my husband and I and our family will celebrate our thirtieth wedding anniversary by dancing at the Lawrence Welks Show—our major concession to the passage of time.

WHAT OR WHO IS AN ECONOMIST?

Webster defines an economist as one who studies and fulfills the basic needs of man. And who, pray tell, is better able to do that than a woman? Seriously, though, the word *economics* is derived from the Greek words, *oikos* (house) and *nemein* (to manage). Managers of households strive to use available resources (labor, supplies, capital) in the most efficient manner to provide for the needs of the family. The same problems characterize the economic practices of the larger units—nations, corporations and businesses. Allocation of scarce resources in such a way as to meet needs in the order of their importance is the key to practicing successful *economics*.

By nature, the role of maximizing family resources has fallen to women; thus, the transition to doing the same thing in the business world should be a natural. Women are born managers. Men make clear-cut, either/or decisions. "Either a new car or a vacation." Women instinctively begin thinking of ways to manage both. Either/or decisions are the antithesis of everything feminine.

The key men or women in business are managers who plan, organize and direct. Managers are a necessity in the business unit. A wise man once said, "The philosopher without the manager has nothing for his supper, ..."

THE BUSINESS ENVIRONMENT

The young lady considering a career in economics must understand the environment in which she will have to work. If her nature is such that she cannot honestly adapt and accept the business characteristics and standards, she should seek more compatible work. First and foremost, business is *competitive*. Competition between businesses is encouraged, and each corporation or business entity fosters a spirit of competition among its employees for promotions, advancement and influence. The woman seeking to enter business must determine whether she likes competition and can stand the pressure which results from intra-office competition. Positions which involve sales and business administration are naturals for the competitive gal. If, for example, she would rather engage in a competitive game (sports, cards, chess) than watch a movie, she would probably do well in business.

Performance, "the ability to produce," is emphasized. The amount of the return in output for each unit of imput is the difference between success and failure for the firm. Therefore, productivity or skill in increasing output is of vital importance, and again pressure is exerted by management to improve performance. If the young lady cannot stand to have people looking over her shoulder or pressure her while she's working, perhaps she should reconsider the decision to enter the business world.

Fast action, too, is a characteristic of the business world. Rapid decisions and rapid change in technology or methodology are part of the business game. Nothing ever remains the same. The woman who resents change, and many tend to, should consider work where tradition and constancy are characteristics. The indecisive Helen or the can't-make-up-her-mind woman are out of place in business, just as the brisk, quick actions of business are misplaced in classroom, pulpit or studio.

Another name for business is *risk* enterprise. The ups and downs of business; the risk taking; the fifty-fifty chance of winning or losing; unemployment risks due to bankruptcy, cutbacks or mergers are risks the employee must understand and assume right along with the employer.

I agree with this description:

> Confidence, fearlessness, the willingness to take a chance and write off losses easily characterize successful women economists. They are optimists, not pessimists. The introvert who worries will never be happy in business, whereas the extrovert will find it fun.
>
> Persistence, the ability to see things through, especially when the going is rugged, is important in achieving results. A sense of timing, of knowing where and when to charge ahead and when to coast along, is another characteristic of successful businesswomen. Some call this talent business discernment; others call it tactful aggressiveness.

In economics, the self-starting ability to get things done is at a premium. Some two centuries ago, Philip Stanhope called this quality "despatch," which he called the "soul of business."

ECONOMIC EDUCATION

The young woman planning to be an economist should decide whether she wishes to concentrate in theoretical or applied economics. In many universities, theoretical economics is taught in the school of social sciences and applied economics is taught in the schools of business administration. For women, career opportunities as a theoretical economist would be severely limited. The young lady might elect to teach economics. Unfortunately, not enough high schools teach economics. Often it is offered as a part of a social science unit with sociology and psychology. Most universities offer majors in pure economics, but the hiring of women professors has been very slow. When I attend professional society meetings, I usually find myself in a rather enviable position of being one woman per hundred men. My economics and business classes, even today, show enrollments which are almost entirely male. Out of approximately sixty to seventy graduate students, three or four girls are enrolled. The only feasible explanation for continued male dominance is that women find other fields much easier to enter and more compatible to their characteristics.

Career opportunities are more numerous in the applied economics field. In the approximately 200 undergraduate schools of Business Administration, women are studying business economics and other forms of correlative applied economics such as office management and office skills (typing, dictaphones, computers and other business machines), accounting (general bookkeepers, controllers, clerks), and marketing (sales, advertising, comparison shopping, consumer economics). Theoretical courses in economics (basic economic principles, micro-and macro-economics, econometrics, etc.) are taught in the major accredited schools of Business Administration. Often, by cooperation between schools, students get their theoretical training in the social science departments and their business training in the business administration departments.

Most universities offer graduate training in economics—the M.S. degree for theoretical economists or the M.B.A. (Masters of Business Administration) for the business economists.

However, there is no statistics to indicate that formal training is an essential ingredient for business success. Experience or a course in a good business college is often a more than adequate substitute. For the young lady wishing to get into business, the best thing she can master in high school is the secretarial skills—typing, shorthand, office machines. With this as an immediate and easy "entrance card," the ambitious woman can look for openings and have an insider's chance at getting them.

CAREER OPPORTUNITIES IN "PURE" ECONOMICS

As was previously stated, career opportunities in "pure" or theoretical economics are quite limited. By the very numbers, then, young women would find it more difficult to find placement in that field where men have traditionally held the few available jobs. Opportunities for the college-trained economist should be divided into three categories: teaching economics in high schools or colleges, working as the economist for a large business or institution, or serving as an economic consultant to business or government.

Teacher

Women professors of economics are still few and far between. I don't know of a single major university where the chairman (or chairperson, as women libbers would have it) is a woman. A recent listing of 700 plus members of a national economic professional society listed fewer than a dozen identifiable women members. When high schools and junior colleges teach principles of economics, it is a part of the business curriculum with major emphasis on office skills. (I got my M.S. degree in "pure economics" and moved onto the university teaching staff as an accounting teacher. Gradually I developed a curriculum with more emphasis on economics and became known as an economics teacher. Later, on a Ford Foundation Fellowship grant, I traveled throughout the United States studying the state of economic education in the secondary schools. It was found to be a sadly neglected area in the curriculums of United States secondary schools. When a grant to work on my doctorate came, I decided to concentrate in the applied economic areas of business finance and investment banking because of the severe career limitations in "pure economics.")

Business Economists

A 1967 study, *Economists in Business* by Alexander, showed that the economist has become an increasingly important figure in the business scene the last few years, both quantitative and qualitatively. The study revealed both the problems and the promises of the professional economist. For example, most economists in business felt that they were not being fully utilized by their employers, but that might be expected in a new profession. Many economists felt they were hired to give "status" to the firm. The answer to the problem of fullest utilization clearly lies both in the growth of management awareness of the value of economic skills and the ability of the business economist to explain himself to a "lay" manager. There is encouragement for economists in both the range, and the changing characteristics of the specialist function which firms have economists perform for them. The growth of corporate planning is a marked feature, as is the increasing need to secure advice on relations between large corporations and governments. Many firms find that economists can perform an interpretative role in this increasingly important relationship. Particularly encouraging is the fairly widely held view that the training which economists receive equips them especially well for objective decision-making.

The growth of the profession has led to the need for techniques, such as economic forecasting, discounting cash flow, statistics, capital budgeting. Many universities do not teach techniques, although their economic training is adequate from an academic point of view. Managers of business, particularly, feel that university training fails to show economic graduates how much of the theory taught could be put to use. The concentration of training in "the higher theory" is often criticized by managers and practicing economists, and it is believed that more concentration on application would be helped. Instead, graduating economists often come from the university with a "box of glittering tools which neither he nor anyone else knows how to use." If a young woman plans to become a business economist, then she should master the techniques and skills which would make her useful in the business environment. Making economists more valuable to businesses, in general, will increase the employment opportunities for both men and women in this area of "pure" economics.

Economic Consultants

The term, economic consultancy, is used to cover an extraordinarily wide range of activities. Narrowly defined, however, it is the study of external economic situations that will affect the firm, together with the implications and opportunities that this economic condition will provide for the client firm, bearing in mind its organization and resources. Much of the consultant's work involves some industrial market research and field surveys, but the purpose is usually to assist the client firm in its marketing or development strategy. Work is also done in the public sector, on the economics of urban growth, regional studies, and the development of industrial complexes. Perhaps one of the most promising fields for the young women is employment somewhere within the vast government complex. More and more, department heads are budgeting for an economist to help provide guidance in developing a social project, or often the economist is there to provide statistics that will justify some pet projects. For this purpose, independent economic consultants are best.

The best bet for the young women economists who consult with firms about their economic future would be to join a consulting firm. Usually she will be assigned to a fact-finding role for many years with the decisions and actual contacts being made by the senior members of the firms—usually males. After many years of experience and when her reputation in the business community is established, she may open a consultancy operation on her own. Often a woman's best route to a consultancy is through a professorship. Almost all of the requests for my services as a consultant originated from students' reports and conversations. Often a firm or institution will contact the local university officials and ask for recommendations for expert witnesses for certain court hearings or trials, etc. where the status of a professor as an independent witness carries some weight. Since a consultant's ability to advertise is restricted by ethics, she must depend upon word-of-mouth advertising from one satisfied client to another.

The opportunities for employment in the pure economic field are improving slowly. Although it has been said, "The Age of Chivalry has gone, that of the economists and calculators has succeeded," the use of economists outside of the university was almost nonexistent prior to the fifties. The phrase *business economist* was coined during the fifties, emphasizing the distinction between those engaged primarily in teaching (academic economists), those applying the art of economics to the government issues (political economists), and those practicing within the framework of business (business economists). As their numbers have increased, the economists have turned to broader vistas and areas of employment.

APPLIED ECONOMICS—A BAGFUL OF CAREER OPPORTUNITIES

The young woman trained as an economist and possessing some practical experience will find a multitude of jobs awaiting the application of her knowledge and skill in the art of applied economics. However, she will not want to start by looking at the want ads. The Sunday edition of a large metropolitan newspaper had forty-eight pages of employment opportunities listed and nary an "economist" job available among all those pages. Where, then, does one look? Look in the pages of auxiliary jobs where her economic training would be of value.

It has been estimated that in the United States there are about 9,000 economists at work. They are to be found working in industrial, commercial, and financial firms; in government jobs by the thousands; employed by special research organization, trade unions and trade associations. Perhaps 1,000 of those are women. Where can the woman economist find employment?

Start a Business

The economist can use her knowledge in operating her own business. There are four basic steps: get an idea; test the economic feasibility of the idea; assemble or know how to get the factors of production needed, i.e. labor, supplies, licenses, permits, patents, sales or distribution programs; and finally, secure the capital needed to begin and run the business until it reaches the break-even point. Women are especially suited to starting a business. As the principal purchasers of goods and services, they must often have said, "Why doesn't somebody do this? . . . or sell that? . . . invent a . . . ? " Each question contains the germination of a new business. Often women can turn hobbies into profitable businesses, and these can be operated part-time or from the home. The young woman economist who wishes to establish a home should turn her attention to operating a business from her home or garage.

Ideas can come from anywhere. For example, a few years ago insurance companies introduced variable annuities. They were ruled securities, which meant that every life insurance agent or salesman would need to pass the NASD (National Association of Securities' Dealers) examination. I called several insurance companies and signed contracts to teach their salesmen how to pass the examination. Again, a few years ago, the newspapers were filled with the economic plight of unemployed aerospace engineers and scientists. We created a corporation and received government funds to teach these men how to start and operate their own businesses.

Get a Job

Other young women trained in business administration and economics should try to find employment opportunities with business, industry and governments. Some of the field she might explore are

Fashion. Since the fashion industry is supported by women, a bright young lady with a flair for fashions can use her natural bent to locate jobs within the industry as a saleswoman, advertising specialist, promoter, public relations, or financial or management specialist.

Publishing. This field lends itself to individual assignments, and since most magazines and large sections of newspapers are devoted to women's activities, women economists find a special niche as reporters on budgets and household management, as finance editors, and in the business management end of running a large publishing firm.

Merchandising. Since women know what induces them to buy, they make excellent salespersons. The want ads are replete with job opportunities—from direct sales in the customer's home to sales representatives for large companies. The young woman with a fresh B.S. degree and knowledge of the interactions of supply, demand and price should become the ace salesperson of her firm. Real estate, mutual funds, and insurance are industries where economic skills would be in special demand.

Office management. An economist should have a thorough knowledge of business tax laws and a mastery of office skills. A combination of these three branches of knowledge should, first of all, open most doors and then allow her to become an indispensable manager of the office and, indirectly, of the business.

Advertising and public relations. The women in this field have increased materially. They can serve as account executives, copywriters, researchers, radio and TV specialists, media selectors, demonstrators, etc.

Computers and statistics. More and more universities are requiring a demonstrated skill in computer programming and utilization and statistical skills. Even small businesses find it necessary to own or lease a computer to handle the vast amount of pagework and records required by management and government agencies. Today everything is being quantified, and the young businesswoman should be sure a healthy portion of her training and knowledge is in mathematics.

Accounting. This specialty is often combined with economics to provide employment opportunities. An accountant is always in demand, and the rapid increase in required accounting record will probably insure that demand exceeds supply for a long time. Interpreting the accounting records to make them useful to management, investment analysts, underwriters, banks, and other credit sources requires an analytical skill which is fostered as one studies economics and hunts solutions to problems of unequal distribution of demand and supply factors.

Government. Governments and their agencies hired almost one-fourth of the nonagricultural labor force last year. Employment opportunities in this are far outpacing any other area. With emphasis on equal opportunities, these principalities offer the best outlet for the young woman economists' talents.

The high school or college coed should take every opportunity to participate in school, church, club or community government. She should cultivate the acquaintance of any government official in the area, pass civil service examinations, and aim for a government job upon graduation. This might necessitate moving unless she concentrates on local governments. More and more government agencies concentrate on economic development, and this field is wide open to women.

The young lady should realize that government work differs in many ways from private industry which is kept efficient by the pressure of competition. In government these pressures are almost wholly absent. Funds for activities are voted by legislatures to whom they must be justified. Primary emphasis is on service to the public, and it is usually impractical to compare the value of the service with its cost. Moreover, government operates in a sort of goldfish bowl; it must account for its actions to a degree which is almost unknown in business. Offsetting unfavorable aspects of government work are relatively high entrance salaries, exceptional training opportunities, job security, and the satisfaction of serving fellow citizens.

CONCLUSION

The common and outstanding feature of the function the woman economists perform in business organizations and governments service is that they are basically of an advisory character; that is to say, they are holding staff functions as distinct from executive or line responsibilities. Economists provide an assessment of alternative choices of action to help decision-makers. The evaluation they offer is made either with reference to special areas of activity or the general policy of the firm and is either connected with external conditions or the internal repercussions that are likely to follow. Lord Keynes, the father of modern economics, wrote, "The theory of economics does not furnish a body of settled conclusions immediately applicable to policy. It is a method rather than a doctrine, an apparatus of mind, a technique of thinking which helps its possessor to draw correct conclusions." Can women function as good advisors rather than decision-makers, i.e. advise rather than tell?

Housekeeping is still the main occupation of American women but no longer the only occupation of most of them. More than half of all women between the ages of eighteen and fifty-five are working for pay. The distinguishing feature of the work of women who are counted as member of the labor force is *money*. They are counted if they work for pay. A recent newspaper reported that sixteen million women now hold full-time jobs, and their medium income is about 40 percent lower than that of man. The college-educated woman earns only 60 percent of the salary given to a man with similar credentials. These statistics may improve with time, but the woman must realistically accept facts as they are now. The Conference Board study showed that among young workers, there is little difference between the salaries of men and women. It becomes then a matter of determination on the part of women to strive to maintain that equality, but she must be willing to accept a disparity in wages without mental distress if it becomes necessary. One way to keep abreast is to constantly upgrade her skills. The working woman has made inroads into professional fields, but, according to the Conference Board, "this does not reflect the opening of new doors for women, but is the result of an increased demand for persons with specialized skills." Some 15 percent of all working women are professionals. Half are school teachers, a fourth are nurses or medical technicians, and a remaining fourth are scattered among all the rest of the professions, including economics and business administration.

As sex-role stereotyping is decreasing in our society, we are realizing that women as well as men can develop the systematic, analytical abilities needed to run an organization. In addition, the interpersonal, intuitive skills that women have already been trained to develop and utilize are basic requirements for smooth organizational functioning.

If you want what you do to have a real impact . . . if you aren't the type of women who is satisfied with a traditional "woman's job," then *become an economist.*

CHAPTER 5

BANKING AS A CAREER AREA
FOR WOMEN

GRACE H. FOSTER

//

Personal Characteristics Important to Success in Banking
Personal Information Relating to the Writer
Discrimination

///

UNTIL COMPARATIVELY few years ago, banking was a profession in which only the male could succeed and rise to key positions with regard to title and responsibility. However, this situation is changing, and more and more career opportunities are being made available to deserving, capable and talented young women. This change is noticeable perhaps more so on the West Coast and, particularly, in California, where women are being utilized to greater advantage and gaining recognition for their abilities as bankers.

Many, if not all, of the larger banks presently conduct training programs within the organization which are open to women as well as men. Depending upon the size of the institution, such programs vary in degree of intensity, since the undertaking of training inexperienced employees is costly to the employer and, in the case of smaller banks, results in additional overhead expense which cannot be justified. As a result, the major banks throughout the country are in a position to provide the most thorough, intense training programs. However, very often after bearing the burden of the expense of training an employee, the bank will lose this person to another institution where, on the basis of training received from the former employer, the individual is in a position to command a better position and higher salary elsewhere. This circumstance occurs frequently and discourages some banks from conducting training programs and making the added investment in an employee which results from his or her participation in such a program.

At one time, women held only menial positions in banks, such as that of stenographer, bookkeeper, or teller. However, today most banks open their officer training programs to women, and these encompass, among other facets of banking, the areas of operations and commercial and installment lending. For those women who are willing to accept responsibility and qualify in other respects, they can look forward to a career in banking that will afford them ultimate promotions to virtually any job within the organization. It must be remembered, however, that not every person is qualified to achieve officer status; in many cases, a woman will, by her own choice, remain a career teller, bookkeeper, stenographer, etc.

Most banks will hire inexperienced personnel and place them in positions to which they are best suited, depending upon any business background that they may have or courses taken in school to prepare them for entry into the field of finance. While training programs vary from bank to bank, they are generally afforded in phases, usually commencing as "back room" clerks and advancing to other positions in the same area that will provide the employee with an opportunity to learn the fundamentals and procedures associated with banking. Upon completing this phase of training, the bank by which I am employed offers the person an opportunity to advance to the position of teller or other similar jobs where they are introduced to and work daily with the public.

Although the classification of teller, note clerk, and statement and safe deposit clerk appear somewhat insignificant, they represent key positions with respect to gaining the confidence and loyalty of the bank's customers. These people are depended upon to represent the bank in a friendly and courteous manner, to provide the most efficient service possible in order to maintain the customers' business, and to provide the basis for a mutually satisfactory relationship.

Considerable experience must generally be gained before an employee is qualified to embark on a training program that will ultimately result in corporate officer status. West Coast banks appear to be more liberal in opportunities afforded women to become officers and, as an example, Central Bank has, during the past three years, adopted a policy to more equitably utilize women in its branches and administration offices. A concerted effort has been put forth to train women for managerial and official positions in the bank's branches and, in 1972, recorded statistics indicated that more than 34 percent of such jobs were filled by women. This compares very favorably with statistics for 1970 which indicated that only approximately 10 percent of these positions in this bank were held by women. A like increase was also noted with regard to clerical positions in the branches which are now staffed approximately 98 percent by women. It can be assumed that such changes, as indicated herein for Central Bank, are also taking place in other financial institutions, particularly on the West Coast.

Employers are constantly seeking bright, new talent to fill available positions. With the changing lifestyle in this country, more and more women are entering the business world, even after marriage; and many employers are finding that women are more loyal and dependable than their male counterparts.

Because banking is offering more opportunities for the female employee, she is willing to work long hours and put forth greater efforts to study and learn. In the field of finance, however, the male has by tradition, until very recently, been the dominating factor. Women are beginning to gain more respect and confidence not only from their employer but from customers as well who, in the past, found themselves dealing primarily with men in their banking relationships, but they must work much more diligently than men to gain this status. This can be accomplished only by excelling in performance and demonstrating equal or better ability and knowledge. Banking and confidence go hand-in-hand, and, heretofore, it was felt a woman could not command the confidence of customers to the extent that they would feel comfortable to sit and discuss problems with respect to finance or other personal matters relating thereto. As women progress in banking, this presumption is proving false, and their equal ability to gain confidence and be accepted by the bank's customers has been successfully demonstrated in the case of Central Bank.

The majority of women in banking achieve executive status only after progressing through the ranks of various clerical positions. However, this has many advantages in that it provides the woman with effective knowledge of the basic fundamentals and procedures and assists her in her own performance, as well as in her direction and supervision of others.

With respect to educational requirements or prerequisites, the young woman contemplating a career in finance or banking should concentrate on business and secretarial courses, including courses in the English language to provide for proper grammar and usage of words. The ability to operate office machines, particularly the typewriter, can be very helpful, since these skills are employed in practically every phase of banking in varying degrees, depending upon the position. The American Institute of Banking (AIB), on a nationwide basis, offers a variety of courses on bank-related subjects. These courses are basic and thorough and generally must be taken during leisure hours and on the employee's own time. Most banks reimburse their employees for any costs incurred when a course has been successfully concluded, which serves as an inducement for enrollment. A college education will generally enhance advancement opportunities in banking, providing the subjects studied are applicable and valuable in the conduct of business. However, in most cases, even the college graduate must undertake some training prior to embarking successfully on her career in banking.

Over the years, banks have been notorious for the low pay scales offered. This is rapidly changing as a result of keen competition for quality employees, and banks are now more competitive salarywise with other industries in order to attract and retain good talent. In addition, many banks now offer complete employee benefit programs which include, among other things, profit sharing, medical and dental coverage, retirement plans, and stock options. These benefits must be taken into consideration when evaluating wages paid by banks since they represent an additional contribution on the part of the employer. In the case of Central Bank, as an example, the cost of fringe benefits amounts to 17 to 25 percent over and above wages paid, depending upon the salary of the individual, and this sum is not subject to income taxes.

PERSONAL CHARACTERISTICS IMPORTANT TO SUCCESS IN BANKING

Integrity

Integrity is an absolute must in banking, particularly since the bank and its employees are entrusted with the care of funds belonging to others. Temptations are many and, depending upon circumstances, it may be relatively easy to defraud the bank or a customer. However, through audits, bank examinations by regulatory authorities, and other means, discrepancies are ultimately uncovered, and the result to the employee involved can be very severe. Any defalcation involving bank funds must be reported to the governing regulatory body, depending upon whether a bank is operating under state or national charter, and must also be investigated by the Federal Bureau of Investigation. When a person is found guilty of a fraudulent act, appropriate penal action is taken, depending upon the amount involved, often resulting in imprisonment. In addition, a person found guilty of a fraud or theft is not bondable, and since many businesses other than banking require for their own protection that employees be bonded, the former bank employee in this circumstance will find it very difficult to obtain other employment.

Many banks have established policies whereby employees are forbidden to accept gratuities from customers. There are several reasons for this, one being that a bank does not wish any of its employees to be placed in a position where an obligation to a depositor or borrower may exist. Such an obligation could result in the employee's being placed in a compromising position where he or she would be expected to grant exceptions to a customer that would be contrary to established bank policies. As an example, a loan officer may accept a gift from a customer and, in return, grant unwarranted credit or afford preferential interest rates or terms for repayment of a loan, all to the detriment of the bank. The uncovering of such a circumstance by the bank could result in the dismissal of the employee.

Honesty and integrity go hand-in-hand and must always be demonstrated and practiced, regardless of the position held in a bank.

Grooming

Good grooming is essential in any job but particularly in banking where so many positions require constant personal contact with the public. It is not necessary to always wear the latest in fashions, but clothing worn should be clean and appropriate, and appearance with respect to hair and makeup should be neat and conservative. Employers realize that their personnel cannot always afford the best in clothing and accessories; however, there is no excuse for wearing clothing that is soiled or in disrepair. It is in the best interests of the employee to exercise good judgement in the choice of clothes, hair style, etc., all of which will ultimately inure her own benefit.

As stated earlier, banking is a public service business, and in every encounter with a customer, one is acting as a representative of the bank. Therefore, it is most important that one be conscious of the obligation one has to the employer and respect the need for a tidy appearance and good grooming at all times.

Personal Behavior

Personal behavior is also very important, both on the job and after business hours as well. Banking, in particular, is a business that commands respect and confidence, and a bank employee must always conduct herself in such a manner that she represents the bank well at all times. This requires that she also demonstrate exemplary behavior with regard to her personal affairs. In view of the need to command confidence and respect as it relates to banking, poor and improper behavior of an employee in public that reflects adversely on the bank, as her employer, can be cause and justification for dismissal.

PERSONAL INFORMATION RELATING TO THE WRITER

Commenting upon my personal educational background and experience, I attended and graduated from public grammar and high schools in the city of New York. As a young girl, I aspired to be a secretary and, accordingly, prepared myself for this profession by enrolling in the appropriate secretarial and other business courses available to me in school. These included, among other subjects, three years of shorthand and typing, in which I fortunately excelled, as well as English, economics and business law. The courses were thorough and, as a good student, I found them challenging and enjoyable which made the task of studying and applying myself to schoolwork less burdensome.

Upon graduation from high school, however, there was very limited employment available, and inasmuch as I was required to work as a matter of necessity in the support of my fatherless family, I commenced my career with a steamship company as a billing machine operator. I was disappointed at not being able to pursue a secretarial career from the onset, but I held the latter position for approximately two and one-half years. I had no training on the job other than my experience as a typist but was taught to operate the particular equipment used in the preparation of ship manifests. Although this position did not provide me with an opportunity to demonstrate secretarial skills for which I was trained, I was exposed to other aspects of the business world and gained experience that I am sure enhanced my future in business.

Upon moving to California, once again employment was difficult to obtain, and I accepted a position with a small, independent bank as a statement and safe deposit clerk. From this position, I advanced to other departments of the bank where my stenographic skills were utilized. However, due to the small size of the bank and limited opportunities for advancement in position and salary, after two years I found it necessary to make a change and accepted a position as a stenographer with the research and development subsidiary of a major oil company.

The almost eight years I spent with that company provided me with very rewarding experience, particularly since the work was highly technical in nature, and the job from the onset was a challenge to my intellectual abilities and shorthand and typing skills. I progressed well with the company by demonstrating efficiency and diligence in the performance of my work.

However, as a result of friendships developed during the course of employment, I maintained a relationship with my former bank employer over the years and, upon realizing the professional experience and background I had gained, I was approached to return to the bank in the capacity of secretary to one of the senior officers. The salary was attractive and the opportunity to now advance in the bank was apparent, since it had commenced internal growth through mergers with other banks and the opening of additional branch offices. Within a short time, I became secretary to the president of the bank, as well as to the board of directors, and this position afforded me an opportunity to educate myself with respect to corporate procedures and permitted exposure to the many intricacies of bank management and supervision. The bank has continued to expand and progress over the years, and, consequently, my job during the past eighteen years has become more and more challenging and rewarding, both monetarily and in a sense of self-gratification.

Presently, I am corporate secretary of the bank and its parent bank holding company, the latter being the first intrastate multi-bank holding company in California. I am also proud to serve as a member of the board of directors of both Central Bank and Central Banking System. In my present capacity, I perform a dual role as personal secretary to the president of the bank, who is also president of the holding company, and also as his administrative assistant. I have the responsibility for many of the corporate and important record-keeping functions of the bank and its parent holding company, and I assist in the supervision of office management of our primary administrative headquarters, which also includes working closely with personnel.

The position I have achieved in our banking system affords me great pride, since few women have been chosen to serve in this capacity with major financial institutions. Our present banking system includes six affiliate banks, which presently operate forty-five branches throughout California, as well as several nonbanking subsidiaries. This diversification adds to the challenge of my work, and, at times, carries me into areas far removed from banking per se.

I feel the success I have attained without the benefit of a college education can be attributed in part to the constant display of a conscientious attitude toward my work and a sincere desire to learn over the years. It required maximum utilization of natural intelligence, which we all possess but do not always apply to our own best advantage. My success serves as a source of encouragement to the younger, subordinate employees who tend to become dismayed with the inconsequential, low-salaried jobs to which they are assigned upon initially joining the bank. I take pride in reminding them that my career in banking commenced as a teenager, with little business experience, serving the bank as a statement and safe deposit clerk, and, from such a humble beginning, I have risen to my present status. It is also evidence of the fact that such success is available to everyone who is qualified and establishes a goal and works diligently and conscientiously to reach it, providing the opportunity to advance is available to them.

Needless to say, I have always been dedicated to my work and loyal to my employer, both qualities being tantamount to success in any field of endeavor. Never losing sight of the fact that life is a continual learning process, I have found in my working years that virtually each day brings with it new experiences and opportunities to be exposed to situations heretofore not encountered that add to my knowledge and experience, thus enhancing my value to my employer. I have always been receptive to objective and constructive criticism and have never neglected an opportunity to broaden my background and knowledge.

DISCRIMINATION

Although I personally feel that women have come a long way in penetrating key positions in banking, it would be unrealistic to state that discrimination does not exist. The female bank employee is being afforded more promotional opportunities at present but, in many instances, women are compensated at a lower level than their male counterpart performing in a position of equal responsibility. However, from experience and personal observations in recent years, I feel this situation will improve in time to a point that, where possible, women will be given equal consideration in every respect.

Statistics accumulated in 1970 indicated that of the nation's 970,000 bank employees, 61 per cent were women, but women comprised only 10 per cent of the banking industry's officials and managerial staffs. It is a fact that women experience little difficulty in obtaining positions with banks, but the jobs available to them are likely to be low-level with limited opportunity for major advancement into key positions. To date, few women have attained managerial or key positions in the commercial lending field or in trust management. The opportunities in these fields should increase as more and more banks open their training programs in these areas to women.

Self-help courses relating to banking, which can assist in acquiring knowledge outside the realm of employment, are offered by many schools and organizations. For example, the American Institute of Banking (AIB), as mentioned previously, offers classes on a variety of subjects relating to banking and enrollment is open to everyone.

One of the major disadvantages confronting the woman in banking, particularly one employed by a branch banking chain, is the fact that women are not as mobile as men with respect to transferring from one area to another. As an example, the bank by which I am employed operates branches throughout the state of California and, oftentimes, women are not receptive to distant moves. This is particularly true in the case of married female employees whose positions are secondary in the household, and a transfer would not be practical or would pose a great inconvenience to the remainder of the family.

Another problem confronting the female in banking, as well as other businesses, is the need to work overtime on occasion. This situation again creates a greater problem for the married woman whose obligations at home preclude her from spending additional time on the job. These factors, among others, will likely continue to act as deterrents to promotions for women in banking.

On the brighter side, automation has opened up many career opportunities for women that heretofore did not exist. This is true particularly in the area of bank operations where computerization has eliminated many physical and manual tasks that were considered excessive for the average female employee. In view of the foregoing, women are now permitted to advance in bank operations, providing they demonstrate the ability and are able to gain acceptance by other women as supervisors. In fact, in our bank, women are proving to be superior in the training and guidance of others and, likely, other banks are gaining the same experience.

Women, more recently, are commencing to enter and be accepted in other fields of finance, such as the investment banking and stock brokerage businesses. For the first time, banks are employing female internal auditors; likewise, regulatory bodies governing activities of banks are commencing to employ women examiners and auditors. This represents a considerable breakthrough for women in a field heretofore open solely to men.

In my work experience, I have observed that it is more difficult for a woman to gain recognition and respect in a position of authority; therefore, she must put forth concerted effort to earn admiration of her fellow employees through superior performance and demonstration of her knowledge and capabilities. Since many men still find it difficult to accept women as counterparts in business, particularly in the field of finance, patience and perseverance are sometimes required until the worth of her services can be appreciated.

CHAPTER 6

CAREER ROLES IN THE MINISTRY

EVELYN STAPLES GRINDLE

///

The Call
General Preparation
Formal Training
Choice of Ministry Type
Ordination
Acceptance of Women into the Ministry
The Woman Minister's Image
Duties of the Pastoral Ministry
Some Fringe Benefits of the Ministry

///

So YOU WOULD LIKE to be a minister? Why not? It can be done you know. It won't be easy, but what really worthwhile investment of life is easy? And anyway, you wouldn't want it to be simple, for that would take away all the fun, lessening the challenge and the deep satisfactions of success.

Everything I read of late about women ministers seems to concentrate on the difficulties involved and places a lot of emphasis on the current Women's Liberation Movement. Now, I am of that advanced age in life where, when I began, I didn't know I wasn't supposed to be able "to make the grade" because of my sex. I was well into my years of parish ministry before I even heard the expression, "Women's Lib." So I just went ahead and did it!

THE CALL

With me it was a recognition of the need in a particular period of history which led into taking the steps which eventually led to ordination and full-time parish ministry. It was at the beginning of the Second World War and our small, local, neighboring rural churches were habitually being supplied by students from a nearby theological seminary. Suddenly the volunteering and drafting of young men were resulting in sadly depleted lists from which the district superintendent could secure leadership for the churches. I found myself "filling in temporarily" in our local church, having held services occasionally through the years since I was sixteen, at times when the minister was ill or on vacation. Then came, what I felt to be, a bona fide call to the ministry, but I did not yet see it as a full-time career for then or anytime in the future. I was at the Methodist Conference in Bangor, Maine, and the district superintendent called me out in to the church narthex and said, "How about taking over the responsibility for your home church for the year ahead and starting in on the Conference Course of Theological Studies?" I was aghast! Then he said these words, and I am sure I still can quote them verbatim, "We need you, Evelyn, the Kingdom of God needs you. Think about it." And needless to say I did just that; "I thought about it" all that long night through on a little narrow, hard bed in a small room in the nearby Y.W.C.A. building. I truly felt the Holy Spirit guiding and directing me and I just couldn't say "No." I think that is how it has to be: a clear, unquestionable "call" for the starting point. You've got to feel the need to serve the Lord in a special way and want that more than you want anything else in the world; this desire has to be more than just a passing fancy; it has to be a deep, gnawing hunger within you which will be satisfied with nothing less than a whole-hearted surrender; and the desire should be experienced over a prolonged period in order for you to be *sure* before taking action.

Any career in which a young man or a young woman makes an outstanding contribution and finds fulfillment and abiding satisfaction and joy has to be one in which he or she feels God had in mind for the individual when He created that person, endowed him with talents and personality traits (and placed him in a certain environment, in some cases). But with the ministry this feeling of rightness has to be especially strong and experienced in depth. For the ministry is a special profession because its first and foremost object is to be God's agent in bringing people into the right relationship with Him and assisting them to be open and responsive to His transforming grace. It has other objects and countless phases and facets and goals and objectives—but that is foremost. So it goes without saying that a girl considering the ministry must first of all be a dedicated Christian with all that it signifies and involves. Jesus told us that the first great commandment is to love the Lord thy God with all thy heart and with all thy soul, with all thy mind, and with all thy strength; and the second is namely this, Thou shalt love thy neighbor as thyself (Mark 12:30-31). I think that about sums it up as to one's choice of the ministry as a career: you must love God and people and be willing to let God use you wholly and completely as a channel for His love and be ready to serve, perform His errands, no matter how monotonous or how difficult or how trying is that service and are those errands, and no matter to whom they need to be extended.

So, if you find you terribly want to be a minister and feel God wants it too, begin to take steps as of now. Talk it over with your minister, with your counselor—perhaps with your teachers—and surely with your parents. This call may have come to you while you were still a little girl, it may come while you are in your teen years—those years full to decision-making—or it may come while you are in college or even into adulthood.

GENERAL PREPARATION

If you have made this great choice, be sure that nothing worthwhile you have done with your life hitherto, or are about to do, will be lost. For if ever there was a profession where every talent, every aptitude, and every experience comes in handy, it is in the ministry. Off-hand I can't think of any subjects you have perused in school, any worthwhile activities or accomplishments but what you will be able to use to advantage at some time or in some circumstances. Surely any work with children and youth such as teaching in church school, acting as an officer and then as a counselor of a youth group will be of incalculable help to you. But on the other hand so will experience in scouting, as a member, or in any graduation of leadership; or work with 4-H Clubs, or what have you. It is very important to learn to relate to people: all people of all ages and walks of life. To learn to really listen to them and to care. This brings up the thought of it's being fine experience for the minister-to-be to early in life to visit the sick, the aged, and to work with the retarded, minority groups, and the economically underprivileged. Perhaps you won't enjoy some of this at first, but you will learn to, and will find it gives to your days great purpose and satisfaction as well as paving the way for understanding and empathy in the professional years ahead.

Then there is the matter of secular work. It helps to know what it is like to earn your bread by the sweat of your brow, it helps to learn to manage your money, to be able to have some to share, some to save, and still meet your needs of every day and for the extras which are most meaningful to you. It is good to read to become familiar with great music and great art; also to have a working knowledge of current expressions of the arts and means of modern communication. And then there are a lot of simple mechanical skills you could be learning that will cause you to bless the day you mastered them, like typing and mimeographing, and running visual aid projectors and tape-recorders. I didn't learn these skills as a young person and it has been an added burden all through my ministry to not be adept in their use.

And then as of now you can start to know your Bible, to read good commentaries and interpretations of Bible truths. This will be a good background for your later theological studies and it will provide you with an ever-growing, ever stronger faith. And that you need before you are exposed to too much questioning and probing of the Bible. Don't misunderstand me; this is not bad, in fact, it is good—if the Bible couldn't stand criticism then is wouldn't be very strong—but you need to have an established faith of your own in the background. Perhaps you will make changes in details of your beliefs, but you will not lose your faith if it is thus fortified.

So now you recognize and admit your "call" and are doing all you can day-by-day as preparation for all that is to be. Now you are ready to procure the very best training available both in the college of your choice and the theological or divinity school. There are many scholarships available for both, and your counselor will be able to help you apply for one or more if you have the need.

I have talked with, and corresponded with, several sister ministers who have attended theological seminaries, and it seems to be the consensus that they do not have great difficulty in being accepted if their scholastic and other requirements meet those demands by the school. In other words, they do not meet discrimination at that point.

Susan Morrison and Mary Kraus writing in *Nexus,* the alumni magazine of Boston University, on "Woman on Mission, New Style" speak of their experience in the classroom thus,

FORMAL TRAINING

Perhaps our greatest frustration was to be found in the classroom. We found that in order to be heard by many of our professors and fellow students, our thoughts must be articulated twice as clearly as any male member. Not only was more clarity demanded, but also a forcefulness and aggressiveness to which we were not accustomed. We soon found this a real struggle. Embracing one's femininity and getting one's idea across was indeed a challenge. The situation has improved greatly, and we find much more acceptance and openness among both students and faculty this year. But it has been a struggle, and we would remind any woman thinking of going into the seminary of that fact.

My friend, Reverend Gretchen Hall writes,

It might be well to share with you my angle on the future of preparation for ministry in a world where everything is changing so rapidly, in education, as elsewhere. Tolland Association (United Church of Christ — Congregational) recently passed a resolution asking that those planning to be ordained by the Association get in a required number of hours in Bible and in church history during their seminary work; this was done because in recent years the old stand-by courses have been neglected in favor of some contemporary activist and other way-out wave-of-the-future theory. I agree with the move, but I also expect there will be a move in the direction of giving a broad opportunity, as the Boston Theological consortium affords, for theological students to follow individual bents and develop individual gifts. So often when a young person follows faithfully the rigid course of studies set up by someone else, he or she finds himself in a blind alley and having his education to do all over. The field of ministry is so broad and the need to keep in touch with people so important for any minister that I'd favor a basic core of old-fashioned theological studies, lots of field work, and sympathetic guidance from a mature minister who was really interested in developing the particular gifts of the individual.

CHOICE OF MINISTRY TYPE

I heard a speaker state that 18 percent of those now entering our Methodist seminaries are women, and the percentage at B. U. is much higher. Now somewhere along the way you will probably decide just which field of the ministry most appeals to you and for which you have the best aptitudes. Of course, christian education has long been accepted as a field for women, and you will probably find little trouble in securing a position in this field or in being fully accepted. Perhaps you are interested in counseling, and I feel that is a field where women, because they are women, have much to offer. Especially if one is later married and has a family which is very important to her. She will be close to the members of her household and will be knowledgeable and sympathetic in regard to marriage problems, communication between generations, and with adolescent and teen-age experiences. A woman is more likely to have had first-hand experience of day-to-day relationships with, and perhaps care of, an older person— perhaps a parent of hers or her husband's. And, of course, she is equally competent in becoming familiar with career planning, helping alcoholics and drug addicts to face their problems, etc. I feel a woman is usually more at ease in a hospital room or by any sick bed. Perhaps this is just speaking in generalities, but I feel women make good counselors. But I understand this field is overstaffed, and it is difficult to secure one's first position, at least. Team counseling with a man and a woman working together would seem to be ideal.

Another possibility is the chaplaincy, which is of course closely related to general counseling and may include the position in some institution or hospital. Another is the career of being a professor of theological subjects. Still another career possibility is that of director of music, and many women with talents in that direction find this very fulfilling for they have the opportunity to work in their favorite field of endeavor and at the same time serve the Lord through the church. An in-depth study of hymns and other religious music is an interesting side-line; of course there is always the composing of either, or both, the lyrics and the music of anthems and hymns or even instrumental music. Although the role of missionary has changed through the years there are still many opportunities for service in this field. Or you might like eventually to serve on a church board at the denominational headquarters in some facet of church work.

That brings us to the parish ministry where I can write from experience as I am beginning on my thirtieth consecutive year in that capacity. And to me "that's it" because here one has the opportunity to use all of the above named skills and to further any, and every, interest she may have. In fact, at least in small churches where you are *the* minister, you will find a call to use *everything* you know how to do and wish for many other skills and much more training. It is in the field of pastoral ministry that we strike the greatest discrimination against women. Dorothy McConnell in "Women in the Church" also printed in the *Nexus* writes,

> Making up about 62 per cent of the church membership, women have no important positions in the policy sessions of the Church. In many denominations they had no place at all until recently. Until fairly recently (and it is still true in some churches) no woman could go on professionally to the attainment of a full status in the ministry. As I write this I realize how rapidly things are changing. Still I am almost afraid to say this lest I be misunderstood: that is, that women professionally can actually go as far in the church as in any other calling. That does not mean that church women are at the same level as men. At the moment there are no female bishops nor are there any, apparently, in the offing. But neither are there any women sitting as justices of the Supreme Court. No woman is head surgeon of any hospital. Even in the field of the theater, where women have had a place almost from the beginning of time; few women are directors or producers. This is true — but it need not remain true. Today women can

go as far as they want to go if they are willing to pay the price. There are still stockades around places of privilege and opportunity, but they are getting rickety.

I, personally would like to add that we have had a woman district superintendent in the Maine Conference; a woman who entered the rural ministry the same year I did—1944. She was forced to retire as a result of a severe automobile accident, but while she served, Reverend Dr. Margaret Henrichsen was very competent as the very first woman with this job.

To continue with Ms. McConnell's statement,

> I want to repeat what I said at the beginning. "Women can take their place in the Church. The atmosphere is favorable for them to achieve anything that man can achieve professionally, given the determination. This implies study, discipline and iron-persistence. This has been required in all minorities. The difference today is that winds are blowing from the right direction.

ORDINATION

Before we go any further with the experiences of being received or rejected which women meet today, I think you might be interested in a brief account of the first woman minister to be ordained in the United States. Antoinette Brown was born in a log cabin in New York State in 1825 and joined the Congregational Church when she was nine, beginning to take part in prayer meetings at an early age. She was graduated from Oberlin College in 1847, where she had been a classmate and friend of Lucy Stone, who was very prominent as a lecturer on the issues of slavery and those of the rights of women. A year after her graduation she returned to take a three-year course in theology, to the consternation of the faculty, community and her family. No woman had ever studied theology at Oberlin before. When she finished her course she was not allowed to participate in the commencement, and for years her name did not appear in the list of graduates for that year.

Antoinette came into national prominence as a leader, with her friend Lucy Stone, in the emerging women's rights movement at the 1850 convention in Worcester, Massachusetts. After an interval of social work, lecturing on social issues, and occasional preaching, she was invited to serve a small Congregational Church in New York. Her ordination in 1853 made her the first woman to receive that recognition in the United States; therefore, she was given considerable publicity by Horace Greeley in the *New York Tribune*.

Although she received the support and friendship of many persons in her parish, trouble arose both because of her sex and her theology which did not accord with the dour Calvinism which was prevalent. She resigned and returned to preaching, this time in a Unitarian Church. In 1908 Oberlin College conferred on her the Doctor of Divinity degree. Antoinette Brown Blackwell died at ninety-six years of age, having lived long enough to see the passage of the Woman Suffrage Amendment giving the vote, for which she had so often spoken. At the time of her death in 1921, the census showed there were more than three thousand ordained women in the United States.*

My ordination as Elder in the Methodist Church was on a mother's day at Annual Conference in Bath, Maine. My mother was present, as well as my husband and children and sister-in-law. It was a day to stand out in my memory for all my days. My children had a little row over presenting me flowers and their aunt had to make sure the flowers were hastily divided into two bouquets. But that was a small cloud in an otherwise perfect day!

ACCEPTANCE OF WOMEN INTO THE MINISTRY

In talking with other women ministers, I have gathered divergent stories as to discrimination experienced. Some say the problem is in receiving consideration on an equal basis with male applicants. One woman told of her experience thus, "I applied by mail for a position which had been called to my attention, applying at first by letter, sending my dossier with my educational qualifications and special interests, and giving an account of my experience which included several successful years in the business

---

*The 1973 United States Census of Population gives the number of religious workers as 227,614 male and 26,062 female; of this number there were listed as clergymen 211, 830 male anl 6,237 female.

world. I heard right back and the response to my application was whole-hearted and warm: my qualifications and training were exactly what was desired and they wished to set up an appointment for an interview. I then signed my full name, having used my initials before as I had been in the habit of doing in business. This put the kibosh on it, for learning I was a woman, the interest cooled off immediately and my qualifications and training were no longer important to them. In fact before we were through, the prospective employer made the remark that he would settle for a less fully trained man before accepting a woman." This I feel is an extreme case, but it is authentic. If only we could get the thought across that there are highly competent, just competent, and incompetent people of each sex. There are still cases when a woman is hired when there isn't salary enough to pay a man for the same workload, but I think equal pay rights are being felt here these days. One woman told me, however, of going to a church where two positions were open; those of minister and assistant minister with corresponding salaries and prestige. She was employed as assistant minister, although the superior position remained open for some time.

Lynda Gregorian Christian also writing in the *Nexus* says,

> We bring this sentiment up to date and ask why the prevailing sentiment in the church appears to discourage women from being ordained, why it prefers to see men as ministers, why most administrators are men, why theology is thought to be a male study, and why the traditional prejudices of the Judeo-Christian religion in regard to women are not attacked with firmness and vigor. No Christian of goodwill today would ever allow himself to make derogatory comments about ethnic minorities — yet this same person would often feel little shame in making his views felt about the intellectual, emotional and professional inferiority of women.

There is no eternal Eve. There are many, many different kinds of women; all are individuals; all are children of God. "There is neither Jew nor Greek, there is neither bond nor free, there is neither male nor female: for ye are all one in Christ Jesus," said Paul in Galations 3:28. This is an ideal of the church which has never been realized. All of Paul's other statements about women have surely found a ready audience, from those ordering covered

heads in the church to silence in the councils. There will eventually come a day when women will be able at last to contribute their
own individual and collective values and insights to a Church and
to a society that have far too long been deprived of their gifts of
mind and spirit.

Sometimes "powers-that-be" who have the duty of appointing
ministers or sending them as candidates to various congregations
are entirely open-minded and recognize the peculiar gifts and
training of an individual who happens to be a woman, and then
finds it very hard to find a congregation to consider her. All of us
women ministers hug to ourselves the thought that we feel this is
fear of the unknown; in almost every case where a congregation
has been served by a woman, or has had real contact with one, it
loses this prejudice and is willing to consider the candidate as a
person.

Getting away from generalities I want to share a few personal
experiences. We had three different women ministers in our
Baptist Church while I was growing up, and I had known four
women pastors in neighboring Methodist and Congregational
Churches, so I went into this blind, having no idea that women
ministers were unknown by many and considered freaks by others.
Fortunately my early years of ministry were all in places where I
was known, and I commuted from my farm home where I lived
with my husband, little daughter, son, and father-in-law. I didn't
strike any active prejudice until the time came when my mother
and I were alone and I was ready for a full time appointment and
to take up residence in a parsonage. The district superintendent
reported that there was a definite unwillingness on the part of
some of the people of the church he had in mind to accept a
woman. The need for a minister had arisen after a crisis in the
church after conference time, and there were not many possibilities he was free to offer. I guess he left the impression "Her or nobody." But he did assure them that they could have a trial period
from then, which was autumn, until conference time in the
spring, and if they weren't satisfied at that time he would make a
change. So with these qualifications, I moved into the village to
serve two Methodist Churches, one there and one some six miles

out. Things went well from the start; I paid attention to business, paid my bills, called in the homes, was a pretty good preacher, and kept the parsonage and grounds neat and didn't have a half dozen or so dogs. These seemed to be the qualifications required. When the D.S. came in April he observed an incident which he loved to tell frequently afterwards. He said, "I didn't find anyone kissing her feet, but I did find a boy wiping her shoes." It was muddy and I had walked across the lawns from the parsonage to the church wearing suede shoes with the then prevalent needle heels, and I had covered them with mud. A high school boy, the son of a woman who had felt that a woman and one of middle age, could never "do anything with the young people" went to get a paper towel and got down on his knees and wiped my shoes, being concerned that I appear at my best for this important first annual meeting. Bless him!

Another experience I had was previous to this in a small rural community where my husband, son and daughter very much shared the ministry with me, and where I had perhaps my most successful ministry. We were all at the Grange Hall working on a public supper to secure funds for renovating the beautiful old church which was in a sad state of disrepair after being closed for twenty-five years. The parishoners did all of the work possible themselves in the repairing. Among the strangers at the supper that night was a lady who said she was an architect, and she was accompanied by her husband, a meek little man with the appearance of being tied to her apron strings. She was desirous of going into "The beautiful old New England church," and someone told her that the minister would go over with her which I straightway did. She was loud in both her admiration and in her suggestions as to what we should, and should not, do as we sought to restore the sanctuary. Finally she said to me, "So you are the minister's wife." and I replied, "No, I am the minister." Then in loud and raucus tones she cried out "Frederick! Did you hear that? *She* is the minister." She couldn't seem to accept the fact. Later when I re-entered the hall the first person I encountered was a very good friend named Fred who was selling the tickets. I told him of my experience and he very dryly said, "Why didn't you send her in

to me, I would have told her, we have become quite resigned!"
I think that sort of sums it up; our people do soon become "quite
resigned" as least, and frequently are pleasantly surprised. It im-
presses me that most congregations once they are sold are very
generous in their willingness to admit that a woman minister is
O.K. I even had a woman say once over the telephone when I
was about to leave a little chapel which had been my second or
third church for ten years along with changes in the others, "If
we were only sure we would get another woman, it wouldn't be
so bad." I laughed and said, "I wish you'd get that on a wire-
recorder; that would be of value to the sisterhood."

Reverend Elsie Gibson who has written "When the Minister is
a Woman" wrote me a recent letter in which she quoted from the
experiences of specific women ministers. She says

> Most of my respondents had faced little discrimination in semi-
> nary, unless they were quite well along in years or went to very con-
> servative seminaries. The discrimination most of them faced in secur-
> ing pastorates is due not so much from administrative officials of de-
> nominations as to the resistance local churches have to the woman
> pastor. But I feel this is changing rapidly. Several people from pul-
> pit committees have expressed real openness to the ministry of women
> to me recently. I think the situation is changing and Women's Lib
> has probably, or undoubtedly, helped to bring about the change. *Then
> she adds this,* "But when a woman gets a chip on her shoulder, she is
> headed for trouble. I know one who has lost two good positions re-
> cently on this account, and another who has gone through divorce
> because her husband could not take her militance.

The American Lutheran Church has recently approved ordination of women to the ministry. This leaves only Orthodox
Presbyterian and the Episcopal Church having registered its resistance to this step within the Protestant Churches, and the
Episcopal has voted to permit the ordination of women as deacons
and the use of "Reverend." In the Roman Catholic Church there
is also deep stirring of the waters. Catholic Sisters now have a very
rich ministry along many lines, everything except administering
the sacraments and for the most part preaching. Reverend
Gretchen Hall writes me that at the World Day of Prayer she attended this year, the speaker was a Catholic Sister and the gather-

ing was in a Catholic Church. And she adds, "Hers was one of the most spiritual World Day of Prayer messages I have ever heard." From this I would suggest that the counseling of young women looking toward the ministry should at least recognize the fact that since Vatican II, significant careers in ministry are open to Catholic women; this would include teaching, counseling, and the conduct of worship.

THE WOMAN MINISTER'S "IMAGE"

I heard a story very recently that I can't seem to forget. A speaker at our Methodist ministers' retreat told it. "A woman minister is like a dog walking on his hind legs, he works pretty hard at it, and often does a good job, but still he doesn't look natural." I think it is up to us to create an image which is received as natural and altogether acceptable.

This leads to the question of the image a woman minister should seek to create. New women ministers are as different as are women in general and as different as are men ministers. There cannot be any stereotyped image. I think each of us should simply strive to be her best self—natural and warm and outgoing. There is always this matter of dress brought up. Most women are agreed on clerical robes for formal leading of worship, weddings, funerals, and other professional duties. But there is a wide divergence in the between-times apparel. Some dress in dark clothes and professional appearing attire at all times. I used to wear black or navy blue when I was mixing with a group of ministers, feeling that bright colors or figured fabrics would be conspicuous. But after looking around at a group of clergy these days, one recognizes the fact that the opposite would now be true, for the clergy even wear pretty, colorful wardrobes. There is a story going the rounds where a man asked a minister this question, "So you are a lady minister?" She answered as if there were a comma after the word *lady:* "I try to be." That has been my object through the years. I have tried at all times to be a lady and to look the part. That does not exclude colorful clothes—rather quite the contrary. It does call for modesty and refraining from extremes in style. In fact I have found that my people, especially those in hospitals and nursing homes, have been particularly pleased to see me dressed in "pretty" clothes. I remember years ago while in my early thirties I was asked to make a call in a nursing home on a lady who was ninety-nine years old. I was a bit hesitant to open the door after her "come in," wondering what in the world I could ever say to start the conversation with a woman of those advanced years whom I did not know! But I needn't have worried, for she noted my flowered hat (we wore hats in those days) and she said, "What a pretty hat you have on; if there is anything I like it is for a woman to wear a becoming hat!" So the eternal woman had taken over and we were off to a meaningful relationship. When I came to one parish where I was a stranger, I was told of two remarks from elderly ladies in the village. One said, "I think we are going to like her because she wears pink shoes." And another said to me, "I'm glad you aren't all dried up." I often wondered just what she expected; a squizzled up little old lady dressed in black, doubtless.

DUTIES OF THE PASTORAL MINISTRY

Any young woman considering the pastoral ministry should have a clear idea of at least some of the many and varied activities involved. In I Corinthians 9:22 Paul writes "I am made all things to all men," and of course he might well have added women and children, for that is about the sum of it when one seeks to define the duties of a pastor. The duties span the whole week, and the hours are long, and at best uncertain, as to the beginning and the ending of each day. So many times one hears "A minister works only an hour or two on Sunday," with the inference that his or her job is thus a snap. I always have the feeling I'd like such an individual to chase one of us around for a week and note his mistaken judgment for himself. No matter how well you think you have planned your program and arranged your schedule you will find that unexpected calls have arisen and you are running late, and are doing just that—"running," plus some hopping and jumping. There is ever a sense of juggling duties, also, and I find myself frustrated often by the feeling that whatever I am doing I have an uneasy feeling I ought to be doing something else. All this is something each one has to work out for herself and will find she is working out again and again as the years go by, for it is all a matter of priorities, and try as you will you just can't be everywhere at once or doing a half-dozen things at the same time, although some of us seem never to learn that. Just to mention a few of the ever-present duties, there is the matter of sermon preparation, working out worship programs, and doing the stencils and mimeographing of bulletins. Once early in my ministry I read, "A minister often feels like the middle of a sandwich; squashed in between two Sundays." It is true that Sundays do roll around with relentless regularity, and I still feel that due preparation for them comes very high on the list of "first things first." And then there are all of the meetings during the week; anywhere from one to four or five just about every day and evening, and most of them need some preparation as well as attendance. There are countless devotions to prepare, and one must be ever ready "to lead in Prayer," lest there be reason for both God and her human listeners to become somewhat bored with her repetition. There are youth group meetings, women's groups, men's groups, family nights, children's parties and picnics, and senior citizens and scouts, and of course, the various administration boards and commissions and committees with which every denomination is blessed. Most of these need a lot of time and preparation on your part of presenting causes and long-range plans and more detailed workings of contemporary activities. Then of course there is teaching to be done: Bible study classes, church membership training classes, and most likely Sunday School classes. Most ministers find themselves involved in various school, civic and social activities limited only by one's time, strength and ability to say "No." I feel a reasonable amount of community activity is good; it provides the minister with the opportunity to make contacts outside of her own particular church group and gives her a better idea of the activities and interests of the pepole in the town where she is working. We have a responsibility and a privilege to take Christianity and the ideals and principles taught by the church out into the world, not depending entirely on the people's roundabout coming to the Church plant seeking these values.

Without doubt, a minister has something to add to the educational and cultural groups in his parish and he or she finds some social and recreational life helpful. But I feel these "extras" have to be constantly watched, and a careful inventory and detailed check made frequently to determine the continuing wisdom of former choices of activities. To get out of things once one has become involved takes more than a little tact, so watch your step in choice of community activities, for your Church program does have to come first. Always so many conferences and minister's meetings and ecumenical meetings, training classes, etc. to be held. There is no end to the paper work—records, certificates, and of course reports and reports in duplicate and triplicate to be sent hither and yon—no later than today.

Then there is the counseling—every minister has a lot of that to do. And the more training you have and the more experiences you have had yourself or have had intimate knowledge of through relationships with other people, the more help you can be in counseling situations. But don't let it scare you; all many people need is someone who is a good listener, someone who gives undivided attention to his complete story and emanates an aura of empathy and true caring. You will find no boundaries in describing your involvement in this type of work, for all ages, both sexes, all economic levels, all degrees of education and cultural background, will seek you out. Along with this will come problems of every conceivable nature. I have been repeatedly impressed how even little rural communities have people representative of all walks of life and surely individuals bearing every type of emotional hurt, and frustration, depression, and unrealistic dream. Once, early in my ministry, a minister's wife said to me, "I shouldn't think people would confide their problems to a *woman* like they would a man." I had had a particularly emotionally disturbing week from having shared some pretty serious problems with several people, and I remember saying. "Then, I guess I'm glad I'm not a *man* minister." Of course, I didn't really feel regret that I had inspired the confidence of those in need; I was just rather floored by it all at the moment. But I do not think that the sex of the minister enters into the situation importantly.

For the most part the person in need is looking for someone to *care*. But I have felt several times that being a woman has made it easier for those who were emotionally upset. This goes also for men who have experienced extreme sorrow or guilt; it is easier for them to find relief through tears in the presence of a woman. For in spite of the great advances in people's being encouraged to show their real feelings, there are still those, especially men of the old school, who are very loath to have another man see them weep, feeling it is weak and effeminate. I know that there have been specific cases in which I have provided a mother image and others that of a daughter and have thus been able to encourage even men to pour out their deepest feelings. Just in passing, although I have felt close relatedness to men in their hours of need, not once in all of my nearly thirty years, has a man of any age or station in life taken advantage, by word or gesture, of the fact that I was a woman or in any way failed to respect my position as servant of the Lord and representative of the church.

Closely related to scheduled counseling sessions is the matter of pastoral calling in hospitals and nursing homes, often and regularly as far as possible. Don't be afraid to be the minister; perhaps you are the only one who reads the Bible and prays with the patients. But I am old-fashioned enough to feel that there is something of special value in visiting in the homes of your parishoners! Every other contact has a stage setting which is often quite contrary to the natural, living conditions of the person or persons. Somehow, once you visit a family in the home and win the confidence of the members so that they share their true life with you, you come to understand their needs in a way in which you can truly minister to the members of the household as a specific unit and according to individual needs and interests. If you can wrangle an invitation to dinner, lunch or supper, so much the better! I could write more than one page about the conditions and experiences of my visits in homes over the years. But I can truthfully say I have enjoyed them all, and I have never allowed myself to be discouraged by disorder or lack of hospital cleanliness and have tried not to be awed and overwhelmed by affluence. *People* live in all of these environments, and I love people—if I didn't, I wouldn't be calling there in the first place.

Funerals call for special ministrations to the bereaved family. It makes it easier for everyone concerned if the minister was acquainted with the deceased and the family. If she has not had opportunity for a previous relationship, it is hoped that she has known about it if an illness has preceded death and has been able to minister to both the patient and the family in this difficult period. If the death has been sudden, the minister should get to see the family at the earliest possible time after receiving the news. It is a good idea to alert your church officers and perhaps others, to the fact that you do greatly appreciate having any illness, death, or other family crisis reported to you. We just aren't as clairvoyant as we often wish we were, and sometimes we just *don't know!* There isn't much you can say or do, really, but your presence is going to be meaningful if you have previously established a rapport—perhaps it will anyway. For somehow we, as ministers, do come into situations as representatives of the Lord in a special way. Cooperate completely with the undertaker, seek to know preferences of the mourners as to details of the service, and then officiate with dignity, exuding your faith in God's love and in the "many mansions" the Lord has gone to prepare for those who love Him. Don't forget to call again, and again, after the service. The following days are very hard, at best, and your prayers and your continuing love and care can make a great deal of difference. Allow the grieved to set the tenor of the conversation and go along with it; perhaps what they need most is to talk freely about the loved one. Perhaps they need words of assurance. Perhaps they desire to talk about other things. Be sensitive to the needs, whatever they are, and pray God will grant you the necessary wisdom to bring the required help.

Weddings are among the happiest experiences of a minister; it is such a joy to share in the happy days of planning, as well as in officiating at the ceremony itself. Seek to make your interviews and counseling meaningful and don't be afraid to be happy with the bride and bridegroom, for we are to "rejoice with those who rejoice" as well as "weep with those who weep." Give just as much religious significance to your weddings as you can from beginning to end, whether they be in the church, home or parsonage, or in this day, "wherever." Many times you will be able to encourage the newlyweds, and perhaps their families, to have a more meaningful relationship with the church. When a new home is being established, there is a good opportunity to emphasize the importance of it's being a Christian home. Other opportunities for like emphasis occur at the time of the birth of the children, particularly if the babies are brought to the altar of the church by the young parents for baptism or dedication. At all of the times of special experiences, sad or happy there seems to be, with many, a sensitivity to religion not experienced in day-to-day living. A minister should always be ready to sense any need for, or interest in, spiritual things, and seek to meet those needs, all the while avoiding being "pushy" and quite literally "turning off" the individuals.

I guess it is only fair to warn girls who are considering the pastoral ministry of some of the extras that they will be expected to do, or they will expect themselves to do, because they are women. For the fact remains that the chief strike against women in the ministry, in my opinion, is that she doesn't have a wife. So you have to be the minister and the minister's wife, both; that carries the implication that you will cook for all of the many pot luck suppers and for the most part make a couple of things for all of the public suppers (and in some cases you'll have two or several churches). Of course, you will try to dig up something for the summer fair and the Christmas sale, the rummage sales and the auctions if your Church sponsor them. And it goes without saying your personal appearance is sort of a command performance. Fortunately, I like rummage sales and auctions, as well as enjoying eating with others as I have to prepare and eat most of my meals alone, and I even like to wait on tables. And, of course, as the woman of the house, you do have to do your laundry, press your own robe, and defrost your refrigerator, and vacuum now and then, and the mantlepiece and the piano always seem to need dusting. You will find you are doing quite a bit of entertaining in the parsonage. Don't hesitate to accept kindly offered help—it adds to your closeness to those who share in the preparation for, and cleaning up after, meals or refreshments. Most of us with hair turning to silver have long since decided we will be wise to employ local youth for lawn mowing and path shoveling, but there is still the matter of flower gardens and shearing the shrubbery, etc. The house cleaning has to be worked in, too, in occasional spare periods of time, but I have never conquered it to the point where I didn't have to take a few days of my vacation time to clean closets and do up curtains. But it's a good change so is "as good as a rest" they tell us, and it is surprising how much more enjoyable these big cleaning jobs are when you can do them with a clear conscience. I have found that having a girl come in occasionally to help dig out the corners is very much worthwhile and makes a "lick and a promise" adequate for a while. But I feel that working with one's hands and bringing out a little perspiration on one's brow through working in the garden or mopping the floor is good therapy and releases anxieties and frustrations more than so-called "rest." When I was a farmer's wife I used to find weeding carrots and picking blueberries out in the beautiful outdoors, even when the sun was hot, a wonderful release of tension after a funeral or difficult counseling session. I am an ardent believer in "I met God in the garden." He is so very close there!

There is something else I feel should be discussed and that is the matter of a woman minister, marriage, and having a family. I'm all for it! I think any minister who has had the common experiences of life is of more value as a minister than one who lives life alone learning of family joys and sorrows by hearsay. I have ministered about an equal number of years as a wife and mother, and then as a widow with my children and grandchildren living out of state. But I wouldn't be deprived of those experiences of living for anything, and I feel they make me much more understanding. Also added to these is the fact that we took care of our parents—my husband's mother four years, his father, seventeen—was with my father in his last illness and then my mother lived with us a total of eight years. In fact my children and my elderly parents have furnished me with experiences to compare with just about all of the problems and joys that I hear about in homes where I call. It is very noticeable that unmarried persons, or those without chick or child, are always filled and running over with advice about how to bring up children and how to care for the elderly. We who have had these enriching experiences are not as prone to air words of wisdom.

Some women marry ministers, and many find a full life in that capacity alone, finding many ways to minister and to fulfill their own creative needs. Surely any training or experience a woman has had in theological training or church work will make her helpful to her husband and his parish. Some ministers have been, and are, co-pastors with their husbands. Some divide the work equally, both teaching, preaching, calling, counseling, etc. while others divide the work more according to their particular interests and abilities. Then there are some of us who married laymen. I was once asked if I felt a woman could continue with her ministry if her husband were not a minister. I said I was sure she could and all the more effectively, but I would warn them she had better pick the husband carefully! Recently, I heard of a girl asked that question, or a similar one, and she replied, "Oh, my husband is liberated, too." A husband under these circumstances must be secure in himself and not given to resenting any popularity or success of his wife's and on the other hand be ready to uphold her in difficulties and build up her ego when it is punctured—as it is at times, and encourage her on "blue Mondays." My husband was always most cooperative in my work as I continued to be with him in his, which was farming. He sang in the choir, transported children—took them from Sunday School and brought back their mothers—helped me when I entertained, took care of the children when necessary, and would even get Sunday dinner and do up the dishes when it was called for. Our children were adopted, so we did not have them as babies. I think it might be well to plan to have a sabbatical year now and then, at least when the babies were small—perhaps a leave of absence for a few years—making sure that you are somewhat active, "keeping your hand in," so to speak. But I feel being a minister offers children many fringe benefits: they learn to meet people easily and learn the fundamentals of courtesy and of entertaining, and they are exposed to many outstanding people and share in many rich experiences. My small daughter fitted into the environment readily and at three was saying, "All the mail there was was some more 'Crusade for Christ Literature'." Her favorite activity with her dolls was, of course, playing wedding, and before school age, she had a very appropriate funeral for the recently deceased President Franklin D. Roosevelt. The son was substituting as Superintendent of Sunday School at ten because "Not one of those women would do it, so I did."

I am sure my children would agree with me that the most meaningful memories we have as a family are built around our shared experiences because mamma was a minister. Of course, the appointive system is a handicap for a minister requiring a permanent residence, and all of my churches were within commuting distance in every direction. I have a sister minister whose husband is a painter, and he could readily make the adjustment, including employment, when they moved. Although a minister puts in long hours and can never depend upon a regular schedule, there are for the most part advantages, and as a usual thing she is able to arrange to be at home to see the children off to school in the morning. And as long as the wee ones go to bed early, she is usually there to hear their prayers and tuck them in before leaving them with their father, grandmother or sitter. Children may attend many services and meetings with their parents and peers—a sharing not possible in many professions. My son would bear witness that he had more pieces of pie than any other boy in the community and more cookies slipped into his pocket after gatherings, and my daughter would vouch to the fact that few professions one's mother might follow would provide opportunity to meet so many boys!

There are organizations of women ministers for the purpose of fellowship and sharing of experiences and encouraging one another. There is a group to which I belong known as "New England Association of Women Ministers" and what was "The American Association of Women Ministers" but is now international in scope and is known as The International Association of Women Ministers. This latter group puts out a very interesting and informative paper called "The Woman's Pulpit." These groups are interested in contacting would-be ministers and seminarians, and they invite any interested to attend the meetings. The girls feel this is a helpful experience as they have the opportunity to know women who are actively employed in many facets of the ministry as of now. And they can ask any questions they wish.

There are several books on the market written by women ministers telling of their own experiences, and in some cases the experiences of other women ministers. There is *Seven Steeples* by Margaret Henrichsen which tells of her experiences in coming to a sparsely settled stretch of Maine which borders on Frenchmen's Bay. She had many and varied experiences which she tells in a way to hold your interest every moment, and she found her clerical life with the stalwart, independent Down Easters rich and satisfying; so much so that she served them for twenty-three years and lived there for a time in her retirement.

"All in One Day" by Dr. Hilda Ives is a fascinating story written by a fascinating woman. Mrs. Ives tells of her call to the ministry and some of her experiences, with the humor which was so evident always. She meant a great deal to so many of us younger women and we lovingly called her "The Dean of Women Ministers." She lived to be over eighty and died on the job.

Reverend Elsie Gibson has written *When the Minister Is a Woman* which is based on the concrete experience of many women ministers who are doing all kinds of work in the ministry.

There is a chapter in *Women's Liberation and the Church*, edited by Sarah Bentley-Doelyon telling of her experiences at Drew and how she felt she faced great discrimination.

SOME FRINGE BENEFITS OF THE MINISTRY

I would like to add a word about "the fringe benefits" of being a minister. There are few, if any, occupations and professions where a person is privileged to intimately share all of the important experiences of life with many individuals and families. It is nice to know of the small triumphs of children and the proud joy of parents, to be shown school papers to admire, to be given school photos as gifts, and to be invited to graduations whether it is your turn to have the baccalaureate sermon or graduation invocation or not. It is even good to be close enough to share the heartaches of other people and to have the satisfaction of knowing you were able to help a bit and to assure your confidants that you will be praying about the problem with them. Then, of course, it is a joy to be one of the first to know of a prospective wedding and have the plans for a new house explained in detail to you long before you attend the house-warming. And what a thrill it is when a parent-to-be or a proud prospective grandparent whispers to you the big secret before it is generally known. Even at a church supper or Sunday School party, it is a joy to have a half dozen or so different children vehemently invite you to sit with them, while they proceed to treat you as "Queen for a Day." I even love being hugged by the half-grown children as I shake hands after church, and to have the tots wave at me in the pulpit while they sit wiggling in their seats. This creates a spirit of rapport between us as I smile back a very personal smile.

How often when facing up to the harrowing experience of saying good-bye to a congregation before moving on to the next charge, I have looked out over a congregation with seeing eyes and thought briefly of the experinces I have shared with almost every one of them during the "tenure of my office." What miracles God has wrought in some of these lives, what miraculous healings, what transformed lives, what definite leadership into vocations and relationships. What courage some of these dear people have manifested in times of pain and sorrow—there was the time that couple's son was killed in Vietnam, the time that family had that awful fire, and that person's prolonged illness when no one knew what the outcome might be. Over there is that mother and her two little children. What a good job she is doing, bringing them up alone after the husband and father deserted them. That family is so loving and patient with their retarded child. There is the elderly man who had to leave home and friends and come into a strange city to live with, or be near, his married daughter—it was a tough adjustment for a while. There is that young person who got mixed up with the law, who has served his time, and church friends have helped the individual get a job and make new friends and build a worthwhile life in the community. Yes, the church can be a "supportive community" in so many different ways, and as the minister you are a part of it all.

I have always taken great pains not to return to previous parishes for professional duties except by invitation of the pastor or under very unusual circumstances, but oh, the joy of returning for a social occasion and greeting so many dear friends and getting caught up with them and the news of their families. There is a special closeness which neither time nor distance eradicates, especially if you make the effort to write some letters and cards and go visiting occasionally.

If you believe you were called to be a minister, continue to pray about it and go ahead and prepare to be one and execute your duties as such with dignity and confidence. Do not be aggressive or on the defensive or limit the enabling power of the Holy Spirit. Don't forget God knows what He is doing, and He did even when He put His hand on your shoulder. And cultivate a sense of humor—how many situations that has bailed me out of —for it is hard for anyone not to have fun laughing at you when you are laughing at yourself, so your "goofs" become a mutually enjoyed joke and "a good time is had by all."

So here is my story of what I feel it is like to be a woman minister. I hope I have been realistic, but at the same time whetted your appetite and challenged you and led you to believe, "God helping me, I can." It requires dedication, discipline and determination, but the rewards are commeasurate with the efforts. It may be trite to say, "One gets out of a thing according to what she puts into it." This is true in the ministry to a certain extent, but it doesn't stop there. You get out of it far more than you put into it, and over and above it all you hope some day to hear the Master's "Well done, thou good and faithful servant: thou hast been faithful over a few things, I will make thee ruler over many things: enter thou into the joy of thy Lord." (Matt. 25-21) And somehow, I don't feel the Lord is going to be concerned about the sex of the servant to whom He addresses these words, do you?

CHAPTER 7

CAREER ROLES IN SPEECH THERAPY

BETTY MURDOCK

W HAT DOES A SPEECH THERAPIST DO? She helps people talk better. Could that be an interesting career?

Already, in the first sentence, we are out-of-date. Many speech therapists do not use that title any more. Earlier, the popular title was speech correctionist and that was descriptive of what they hoped to accomplish. Some were called speech specialists or specialists in language or communication disorders or some such combination. In some parts of the country "clinician" was the term. Now most such professionals are called speech pathologists.

Why do people need someone to help them talk better? What can be wrong with the way people talk? Who needs help? Speech problems come in an infinite variety of disorders, symptoms, causes, and degrees of severity. All kinds of people need help.

Stuttering is probably the most dramatic of the common speech disorders. The stutterer may repeat the first part of a word, he may repeat the whole word, he may prolong a part of a word, he may omit words, he may add unnecessary words or sounds, or he may have long silences where nothing comes out. In addition to these "primary symptoms" which can be detected by listening, the stutterer may also have "secondary symptoms" which make his speech "look bad." His inner struggle to express himself may manifest itself in facial contortions. He may try to "force out" his words with hand gestures, foot movements, head jerkings, eye blinkings, and what not. He needs help.

Articulation problems constitute the bulk of the "case load" of the public school speech pathologist—the child who says, "The

101

bwown wabbit was wunning down the woad," or "I thaw thix bithycles thpeeding patht," or "Yook at the yitto yamb." Some parents and teachers ask, "But won't he outgrow his baby talk?" He *might,* and an experienced speech pathologist will be able to make an educated guess about that. But, incredible as it may seem in this age of television, many children come to kindergarten with *every consonant* sound wrong, either substituting another sound, distorting the sound, or omitting it. No one can understand a word they say. Even three or four misarticulated consonant sounds can make a child's speech almost unintelligible. Meanwhile, his personality is being warped through frustration and misunderstanding, and he is falling behind in reading, spelling, and language arts. He needs help.

Voice problems range from minor to serious. A deviate voice can drive a constant listener up the wall. The voice may be nasal (talking through the nose), denasal (as if one had a bad head cold), too loud (nerve-wracking), too soft (hard to understand), aspirate (breathy), too high or too low in pitch to be appropriate for one's age and sex, or hoarse. Many of these voice problems need medical attention instead of or in addition to speech therapy. Hoarseness, for example, may be caused by vocal nodules which may be the result of misuse of the voice. Little league baseball could be the culprit here.

Examples of speech and language disorders which have their bases in physical anomalies are (1) problems of the deaf and hard-of-hearing (a child is not likely to learn to speak properly without special training if he cannot hear well enough to imitate speech sounds), (2) cleft palate (part of the roof of the mouth may be open so that some of the sound goes out through the nose instead of through the mouth), (3) cerebral palsy (the affected child has poor control over the speech mechanism), and (4) aphasia caused by injury or stroke (the victim may have to go through the whole process of learning to speak again).

Speech therapists may also be language specialists and are frequently called upon to give help with such problems as (1) English as a second language, (2) foreign dialect, (3) delayed language development (the child is slow in learning to speak), (4) childhood aphasia (the child does not learn language in the normal way and will need special training), (5) autism (the child does not relate to other people in a normal way), and (6) the child who does not talk at school.

Speech problems are often found in conjunction with personality problems. It is difficult to say whether the speech problem caused the personality problem or was caused by it. The two form a vicious cycle, and the symptoms are soon inextricable. The child's feelings toward his speech problem are part of the problem.

Sometimes the speech problem reflects a larger family situation. The family that yells a lot (perhaps with a television set, a radio, and a stereo going at all times) need not be surprised if one or more of its members develops a hoarse voice. Military type fathers (who think that a family can be disciplined like an army camp) and perfectionist mothers sometimes find that they must relax a little in order to help a child overcome a speech problem. The speech therapist may need to interpret family life-styles in terms of their effects on the speech and language of the children. The therapist may have difficulty in convincing the mother who wants to help her child that "correcting" him every time he says the wrong sound, even before he has learned to make the correct sound, may upset him so much that he will regress rather than progress. Parents are often surprised to learn that they can best help their child by *listening* to him. Listening may be a new role, especially for the father, and one for which he has no talent, time nor patience. Pointing out these home situations to the parents is difficult (they want to do all the talking), but getting them to change life styles is well-nigh impossible.

So lots of people need help with speech and language disorders; but is speech therapy a good career for a girl? Yes, it is. Many professionals in the field right now are young women recently graduated from college. One does not need to be big, strong, or fast in order to be a good speech pathologist, so, perhaps a girl will not be aced out by a man just because he *is* a man. A girl may have a little edge in the field because she may be willing to exercise more patience and attention to minute details than will many men. Minority girls are welcome in the field of speech pathology, and a *true* bilingual background can be a real asset. Girls in wheelchairs have been very successful in the profession.

A certain amount of discrimination still exists in speech pathology as evidenced by the fact that many supervisory positions are still held by men, many of whom have no training whatsoever in speech pathology but have been put in charge of special programs because they have public school administrative credentials. The situation is improving and is no worse and probably a little better than it is in other professions.

If a girl is intelligent (the college courses are not easy), interested in helping people, willing to work hard, capable of self-direction (a therapist is on her own most of the time), and has excellent speech and a superior command of the English language, then she can be a successful candidate for a career in speech pathology. If even one of these qualifications is missing, then perhaps she should consider some other career.

Knowing that she has the proper personal qualifications, how does a girl train herself to become a professional speech pathologist? College is the only way, and there are no shortcuts. Colleges and universities have their own programs and standards, and the various states have specific requirements for certification for speech and hearing specialists in public schools, and some have licensure laws for private speech therapy.

The American Speech and Hearing Association (to which most speech therapists belong) issues Certificates of Clincal Competence in speech pathology and in audiology (the science of hearing). A certificate of clinical competence is not usually a requirement in obtaining state certification or in obtaining a position as a speech therapist; but if one has these qualifications, she will probably be able to meet the requirements of any state or institution.

The *ASHA Journal,* Volume Fifteen, Number two, for February, 1973, carries an article on pages 77 to 80 entitled, "Requirements for the Certificates of Clinical Competence." This article should be studied very carefully by anyone interested in a career in speech pathology. It suggests that one's general background education should include studies in human psychology, sociology, psychological and physical development, the physical sciences, human anatomy and physiology, including neuroanatomy and neurophysiology. One must have sixty semester hours of studies dealing with the normal aspects of human communication, development thereof, disorders thereof, and clinical techniques for evaluation and management of such disorders. Twelve of these sixty semester hours must pertain to normal development and use of speech, language and hearing. Thirty of these sixty hours must be in communication disorders and the evaluation and management of speech, language and hearing disorders. Twenty-four of these thirty semester hours must be in the professional area (speech pathology or audiology) for which the certificate is requested. Thirty of the total sixty semester hours must be acceptable as graduate courses.

Besides the college courses, an applicant for a Certificate of Clinical Competence from the American Speech and Hearing Association must have completed 300 clock hours of supervised clinical experience with a variety of communication disorders. This experience must have been obtained within his training institution or in one of its cooperating programs.

After completion of the academic and clinical practicum experiences the applicant must do the "clinical fellowship year," nine months of full-time professional experience in which bona fide clinical work is accomplished.

After completing the clinical fellowship year, the applicant must pass either the national examination in speech pathology or the national examination in audiology.

In order to apply for the certificate of clinical competence, one must be a member of the American Speech and Hearing Association.

After having accomplished such a formidable training program as this, what career opportunites will be available? The speech pathologist may work in a variety of settings. Most of the job opportunities will be found in public schools, but many other positions will be open to a well-trained therapist. Private practice is quite rewarding in certain locations. Many orthodontists like to refer their patients to speech therapists for work with tongue thrusting which may or may not involve a speech problem. Private clinics are becoming more numerous. University clinics need professional supervision, and university classes are taught by trained professionals. Some hospitals have speech therapists on their regular staffs. Various positions are available for audiologists.

Besides fitting one for a specific position in speech correction, training in speech pathology could be helpful for teachers of exceptional children in various areas. Many school districts operate special classes for mentally retarded children, those with educational handicaps, aphasic children, and those who are deaf and hard-of-hearing.

The most likely position for a girl with a brand new credential in speech pathology will be that of public school speech correctionist. And what does a public school speech correctionist do?

At the beginning of the school year the speech therapist must use some kind of screening process for the purpose of identifying the pupils who need help with communication problems. Frequently, a therapist will give some kind of a speech test to all children at certain grade levels, for example, first, second and third grades, and then depend upon teachers in the upper grades and kindergarten to refer children who seem to need speech help. This speech test might be a series of pictures for the children to name, these names encompassing all the consonant sounds in the initial, medial and final positions in the words. While the pupil being screened is naming these pictures, the therapist will also be listening for clues to such things as stuttering, hearing loss, voice problems, deficient vocabulary, other languages, etc.

Such a screening and referral system will produce a long list of pupils needing help with speech and language problems. It is a good idea at this point for the therapist to confer with each teacher and tell her exactly what she found out in the testing process and to ask the teacher to add any pertinent information which she might have. Then the therapist must use her professional judgement in selecting her "case load" and resist pressures from parents, administrators and teachers to "take just one more." Selection is usually based on the philosophy that one works with the pupils who are most in need of help. The case load should be limited to a definite number; for example, the state of California will reimburse a school district for operating a speech correction program, but the therapist may work with no more than ninety children in any one week.

After the pupils who are going to receive therapy have been

selected, the speech pathologist makes up a schedule which must take into account some or all of these complexities: (1) groups should be composed of children of approximately the same age and grade level and with approximately the same kind of problem; (2) children whose problems are unique in their school or at their age level or who are unable to work in a group because of behavior problems will need to be scheduled individually; (3) some children will need to be scheduled only once a week, some twice a week, some more often; (4) which school(s) to serve on which day(s) of the week (a public school specialist will usually serve more than one school) ; (5) different bell schedules for different schools and for different grade levels within a school; (6) sharing a room with another specialist such as a psychologist or reading specialist; (7) multiple lunch hours; (8) children who are scheduled out of class for other subjects such as remedial reading or instrumental music; (9) "staggered" reading schedules in which half the children come for reading class from nine to ten o'clock in the morning, the other half arrive at ten o'clock and study other subjects with the full class; at two o'clock the "morning readers" go home and the "afternoon readers" remain for reading class until three o'clock; (10) "double sessions" with some students attending school in the morning and some in the afternoon; (11) "year-round-schools" in which the pupils are divided into four groups geographically and each group goes to school for forty-five days and then goes on vacation for fifteen days; one-fourth of the children are on vacation at any given time and the speech schedule changes every three weeks. The speech pathologist who can arrange a schedule to suit everybody is indeed a miracle worker.

While the schedule is in process of being "shaken down" or possibly beforehand, many therapists will be conferring with parents and teachers, arranging with nurses for hearing tests (or doing audiometric testing themselves) , doing further diagnostic testing for some students and making arrangements for school psychologists to do further testing for certain pupils. Nurses may also help in arranging for further medical attention such as laryngoscopic examinations (an ear, nose and throat specialist looks at the vocal cords) for students with hoarse voices.

As therapy sessions get underway, a speech pathologist must

plan and carry out a program of remediation for each pupil. She must decide which methods to try and have alternative methods in reserve in case the original plan does not work.

In many school districts, several speech therapists may have to share materials and equipment, so cooperation among colleagues is absolutely essential. Some kind of filing, storage, purchasing and check-out system must be operated by the group in order to keep the materials in usable condition.

One of the most difficult problems of the speech therapist is having the proper materials and equipment on hand at all times. She must plan ahead and carry these about with her from school to school, sometimes because she has only one of a certain item in her possession, and sometimes because she has no safe place in which to store equipment in some of her schools.

Equipment of the more permanent and expensive kind (known in school districts as "capital outlay" items) used generally by speech pathologists include (1) tape recorder, (2) record player, (3) filmstrip projector without a fan (quiet is absolutely necessary in a speech therapy environment and fans are not quiet), (4) tape recorder which plays a loop tape designed to play back automatically in four to eight seconds, (5) audiometer for testing hearing (usually shared with the nursing staff), (6) casette type recorder with automatic stop and push-button go for prerecorded lessons, (7) machine with a meter indicating whether or not a person is speaking a correct "s" sound into a microphone, (8) diagnostic tests, (9) silent portable heater.

Speech correction materials in general use are (1) workbooks for various sounds, (2) drill books, (3) story books, (4) picture story books, (5) pictures, (6) card games, (7) board games, (8) records, (9) tapes, (10) film strips, (11) flannel boards, (12) small plastic objects, (13) tissues (speech students have a lot of colds), (14) teacher-made materials, and (15) a clock.

Space is sometimes a problem for the public school speech pathologist. Many public schools were built before any kind of special services were offered in schools. The space available in an old crowded school may be a broom closet. A therapist may need to be a little pushy in order to obtain proper facilities in which to carry on a speech correction program. A small room is best because nobody else wants it, and it can be your very own. It should be furnished with a teacher's desk and chair, filing cabinet, table, chairs, a wall mirror, storage space, electrical outlets, silent heat and ventilation, adequate lighting, darkening drapes for filmstrip viewing (if, indeed, the room happens to have a window), carpeting, and soundproofing. A therapist may dream wistfully of a place to hang up her coat.

A central location in the school is important for the speech room because most therapists walk around to pick up students from their classrooms. Classroom teachers have too many other things on their minds to remember to send students to speech class once or twice a week, and a therapist will waste more time waiting for a student to arrive late for speech class and wondering whether he is absent than she will lose in picking up students from their rooms. The walk down the hall every half hour or so will also keep the therapist from going stir crazy in her broom closet and is a fine time to gain rapport with the group, hear what important news they have to tell, and get everybody ready to start the lesson as soon as they enter the speech room.

What does the speech correctionist do during the therapy session to help the child talk better? Every therapist develops techniques which work for her and for the children in her program. A therapy session might be something like this for four second-grade children who have been substituting *th* for *s*. The therapist might read or tell a story about how Sam Superboy rescued Susan Sweetheart from the wicked Sylvester Sinister. The children clap their hands every time they hear a word that starts with the *s* sound. They might also hiss the villain. The children will probably need some ear training in hearing the difference between *s* and *th*. The therapist can give a series of words like *think* and *sink*, *thing* and *sing*, *thick* and *sick*, and ask the children whether the first or second word started with *s*. Then the children might practice producing the correct sound in isolation in various ways like loud and soft, short and long in groups of two, three, or four, *etc.* Then they might practice the *s* with various vowel sounds like *say, see, sigh, so, Sue.* They may be ready for words, phrases and sentences and could perhaps practice them on one of the electronic devices which either plays back their words or indicates on a dial whether or not they have produced a correct *s* sound. Another type of drill might be holding the beginning *s* until the therapist gives a signal and then finishing the word, saying, *"sssssss* (signal) *un, sssssssss* (signal) *oup,"* etc. The therapist might give a word such as *rope* and ask the children to think of a word that rhymes with *rope* but starts with *s*. They will, hopefully, respond by saying, "soap." When the *s* has been firmly established in the beginning of the word, the children will be ready to work with *s* at the end of the word, in the middle of the word, and finally with *s* blends like *spool, start, sled, skate, spring, scrap,* etc. Children love to work with tongue twisters like, "She sells seashells by the seashore" and little rhymes and jingles like

> Summer's such a super time
> We swim and splash till suppertime.

If all has gone well, the therapy session might end with a card game such as Concentration®, Go Fish, or Rummy, using matched pairs of cards with pictures of things with the *s* sound in their names. Each player will use the names on the cards many times during the game. The game is usually a reward for good work during the speech lesson, and it works like a charm.

Some states pay extra money to school districts for the operation of speech correction programs; therefore, somebody has to keep track of how much time each student spends in speech class. This attendance accounting usually becomes the duty of the speech pathologist, and she must keep a record of how many minutes each student spends with her each week. Monthly and annual reports can be complex, but a fair grasp of the concepts of basic math will carry one through.

A successful speech therapist must operate a continuous public relations program, keeping everybody informed about what is going on in the speech room. Parents, teachers and administrators need to know how the speech program enhances the total educational program. The speech therapist and the reading specialist can help each other by trading information about their mutual pupils and by respecting the other's scheduling problems. The school nurse can be a valuable liaison with medical personnel, especially pediatricians; ear, nose and throat specialists; orthodontists, and dentists. Speech therapists and psychologists usually work very closely in helping to plan special programs for children with speech, hearing or language problems. Frequently conversations with colleagues in these closely related professions will help the busy speech therapist keep up with what is new in medicine, dentistry, psychology, and special education that pertains to her field, and also gives her a chance to reciprocate with information of value to her colleagues.

Keeping up with new research is important for speech pathologists, as it is for all professional people. This can be accomplished by reading the journals, attending conferences, and taking short courses and seminars. One can also learn a lot by supervising student speech therapists.

A speech correctionist must be able to drive a car because she will probably serve in more than one school and will possibly need to change schools during the day. Some districts will reimburse the therapist at a modest rate per mile for driving her car between schools.

Speech correction has other monetary rewards. Rumor has it that some private speech pathologists make a lot of money. The salaries of public school speech therapists are comparable to those of teachers in the same area, although the therapist may be paid something extra for working extra time. She may have completed more college work than the average teacher and therefore be higher up on the salary schedule. Certain districts do not pay extra salary for extra degrees; for example, a person with a Ph.D. degree might be paid at the same rate as a person with a Master's Degree with comparable experience. It will behoove a new speech therapist to join her local, state and national teacher's associations and to work with them in solving problems such as salary and working conditions.

It sounds like a lot of training for a fine career, but suppose the young lady changes her mind and decides to get married and raise a family. Won't it be a terrible waste? No such thing! Nothing could be better for a marriage than to have at least one expert (preferably two) in the psychology of communication. And very few activities in life are more fun than teaching your own baby to talk, a possible exception being teaching your grandchild.

CHAPTER 8

CAREER ROLES FOR FEMALES IN PSYCHOLOGY

CECILY GRUMBINE

///

The Academician
Clinical Psychology
Community Psychology
Consulting Psychology
Educational Psychology
Engineering Psychology
Environmental Psychology
Experimental Psychology
Industrial Psychology
Psychometrics
School Psychology
Social Psychology
Newer Areas of Psychology

///

So YOU THINK you might like to become a psychologist? When I was your age I thought so, too—and still do! Moreover, since I am also a female, like you, and am practicing in the field of psychology, perhaps I can answer many of your questions as you consider choosing psychology as your life work.

First, I suspect, you might be wondering just what is a psychologist? A psychologist has been defined in many ways, but I believe the following definition includes most of what a psychologist is:

"He is a scholar, committed to increasing man's understanding of himself and others, and a professional practitioner applying his scientific knowledge in the service of the welfare of others."

How well do your goals match these? Are you interested in involving yourself in these two ways? Your answer to these two questions should help you begin to decide whether you might like to become a psychologist.

The large majority of psychologists in America apply their professional talents in institutional settings: clinic, community, industry or school. A small minority are self-employed, working in essentially unsupervised private practice settings.

How Can You Identify a Psychologist?

First of all, a psychologist is someone who has completed the training and experience recognized as necessary to perform the function consistent with one of the several levels in a career in psychology. This training demands possession of a degree earned in a program primarily psychological in nature. You must anticipate remaining in school for a long period of time, at least until you gain the master's degree, but preferably the Ph.D. or the Ed.D., to be recognized as a psychologist.

How Does the Psychologist Differ from the Psychiatrist?

The psychiatrist is a physician whose degree has been earned in a program primarily medical in content. Hence, the degree he earns is the Doctor of Medicine (M.D.) which permits him not only to work with people with problems but also to recommend and prescribe drugs to help improve the functioning of the individual who is emotionally disturbed. However, he generally limits his practice to working in his office with individuals or sometimes groups. The psychologist, on the other hand, employs his talents in a much broader way, not only acting as a therapist to individuals and groups if he is a clinician, but also applying his knowledge and experience in many other settings and many other ways. (We will discuss these in more detail later in this chapter.)

Are There Any Similarities Between the Two Professions?

Certainly. As you may now be aware, the professional in either field is concerned with the person with a problem. Both provide services for a fee. Both must be registered appropriately. Both must be certified or licensed according to the laws of the state in which the individual will practice.

How Does One Obtain Such Certification or Licensure?

Many states now have laws outlining how one can be certified or obtain a license. In the absence of such laws, the state psychological association may take the responsibility of certifying to the adequacy of an individual's educational training and experience.

What Are the Usual Requirements for Certification?

In the case of both the psychologist and the psychiatrist, earning the necessary degree is only the first step, to be followed immediately thereafter by an internship or practicum training or other supervised experience. For example, in the state of Colorado, the psychologist must spend two years under the supervision of a licensed psychologist before he may practice on his own. Only then is he considered adequately trained to engage in practice, whether in a clinical, industrial, military, school, or other applied setting.

Is There Any Other Recognition for a Psychologist?

Yes. The American Board of Professional Psychology (ABPP) was established to certify that the individual awarded one of its diplomas (the ABPP diplomate) has demonstrated superior competence in his specialty. This is usually determined on the basis of an examination including a practical situation typical of the setting in which the psychologist is engaged. There are now four specialties for which the ABPP diploma is presently granted: Clinical Psychology, Counseling Psychology, Industrial and Organizational Psychology, and School Psychology.

What Training Is Needed to Climb the First Rung
of the Ladder Toward that Goal?

As you have probably surmised by now, you will be required to earn a bachelor's degree at an accredited college or university before going on to graduate study. At some schools you may be able to skip getting the master's degree in order to proceed directly to your doctorate. Other schools may suggest that you get the master's degree first, so that you may be able to begin work in the field in case you cannot see your way clear financially to continue immediately toward the doctorate.

Obviously, to get that much training requires a lot of money, especially in these days of rising costs and a devalued dollar. You must either have chosen your parents wisely (i.e., they must be very rich!) or you must seek other sources of financing your education.

How Can One Obtain Financial Aid?

Fortunately for you, funds are available to help you acquire the training you will need, but you will have to seek them diligently. A major student reference providing information about student aid is *Scholarships, Fellowships, and Loans* by Dr. S. Norman Feingold, published by Bellman Publishing Company, Arlington, Massachusetts 02174.

Most students find that a combination of methods of financing is necessary. Few can depend entirely on only one source. Most report that the financial contributions of their parents, augmented by their own earnings, were the principal forms of financing their college education. Although more than a quarter of those attending college receive a scholarship, this was only a minor source of funds for paying their way through school. The main source was part-time work during the school year while attending college, and full-time work during summer and Christmas vacations.

Which Schools Provide the Best Advanced Training in Psychology?

If you have not been intimidated by the many requirements you must meet before you can function as a psychologist, you are probably wondering where you can get the best training. In a study made in 1970 the ten top institutions for training in psychology were Stanford University, the University of Michigan, the University of California at Berkeley, Harvard University, the University of Illinois, the University of Pennsylvania, the University of Minnesota, the University of Wisconsin, Yale University, and the University of California at Los Angeles.

What Courses Would Be Helpful in High School?

A good college preparatory program would be most helpful in high school. This means that you will want to include English, history, a foreign language, science and mathematics. These are not hard and fast requirements but will provide a good foundation for your future study. The quality of the work you do will be as important as the particular courses you take. However, if you are particularly interested in psychological measurements you should take and enjoy two years of science and three of math to increase your chances of interest and success in that area of work.

What Courses Would Be Helpful in College?

When you get to college, your program should, of course, include psychology, with attention given to child psychology, the psychology of adolescence, social psychology, principles of psychological measurement, and clinical psychology. In addition, you should include a wide variety of related subjects, such as economics, sociology, philosophy and education. Last, but not least, you should elect courses in other areas, including English and foreign languages, to help round out your general education.

Which Courses Are Most Likely to Enable One to Get a Job?

Over and above the courses required in any psychology program you will probably find that courses in communication and management are most likely to enable you to get a job. General cultural and general science courses are least likely, despite the fact that personnel officers say they want a well-rounded individual. In any event, you would be somewhat better off in the job market if you were to take a few courses useful in the business world or closely related to job requirements.

At the same time, you should take advantage of any opportunities for travel as well as a variety of courses in school because they will contribute to the development of a broad background which may assist you to understand and empathize better with your fellow students now and your colleagues, patients and clients of diverse backgrounds later on.

How Can One Determine If She Should Consider Psychology as a Vocation?

Because of the tremendous cost and long period of training required, an individual who plans on entering the field of psychology should be certain that she has both the motivation and the qualities necessary for success as a psychologist.

Many individuals take courses leading to work in psychology because they have problems of their own with which they want help. If this should be part of your motivation, be aware that it is acceptable so long as it is clear to you and you do something about it, i.e. go into therapy yourself to resolve your problems before trying to help another with his.

Your aptitudes are also important. The most obvious of these is skill in human interaction, an ability to listen creatively to another. You may get some idea of how well you do this by looking into your past to see if people have come to you spontaneously because you have proved a willing ear, helpful to them.

Obviously, you must also have scholastic competence to enable you to maintain an adequate grade average in your studies over a long period of time, especially at the graduate level where competition is the name of the game.

Also necessary is a sincere interest in people, since they will be the "stuff" with which you will be working. Your entrance into the field of psychology should be the result of a need on your part to be of service to your fellow men. Whatever your other motives, this is a "must" because service is the basis of the work done by the psychologist, whose major concern must be attending to others' needs and welfare in personal ways.

Yet at the same time, you must meet your own individual needs so that you may experience personal fulfillment and gain the satisfaction of being a member of this profession. Only then can you set forth to maximize your potential contribution.

If One Decides to Enter the Field of Psychology, Are There Options Available in Terms of Areas of Interest?

Most certainly there are. As suggested earlier, you might, for instance, work as a clinical psychologist, helping individuals who apply to your clinic for resolution of their problems. Or you might teach at the junior college or college level as an academician. If you enjoy working in a laboratory, you might become an experimentalist with animals, while, on the other hand, if you prefer rubbing elbows with the rough and tumble world you might opt for social psychology. In recent years, whole new areas have opened up, among these being work with interested leaders in the community, fostering community mental health.

How About More Details On Each of These Areas?

They are given below in alphabetical order for your ease in finding the area in which you are most interested. Also, although men are presently the chief workers in all of these areas, because this book is being written for you, the young female, the feminine pronoun has been used throughout this chapter.

THE ACADEMICIAN

The psychologist whose interest is in teaching is often called the academician, especially if she functions within the psychology department of a college or university. Seemingly her field of specialization depends on sex differences, but may be the result of discriminatory practices, the male professors preferring general and experimental psychology and consequently appropriating those areas, leaving the women to go into the remaining areas—clinical, counseling and guidance—whether they prefer them or not.

Quite clearly, if you are interested in this field, you should enjoy teaching, since you will be spending your working day attempting to transmit your knowledge to the younger individuals who will be your students.

As a woman, you are likely to find the opportunities for college teaching less available to you than to the men. This sex difference has been increasing in the recently tightening job market. For example, a new college on the West Coast recently had 5,600 applications to fill its initial thirty academic positions! In addition, you will have to be able to accept the fact that in academic rank, salary, and tenure you will be at a disadvantage compared to the men.

CLINICAL PSYCHOLOGY

If you become a clinical psychologist, you will deal with the psychological problems involved in the diagnosis, treatment and prevention of mental illness and emotional disorders. You will conduct psychological examinations which will include obtaining case history data by personal interview. You will also use psychometrics, such as intelligence tests, and may in addition employ projective techniques, whereby the psychologist taps the subconscious level of the subject in order to gain a better understanding of him. After analyzing the facts obtained in these examinations, you may then recommend corrective programs. These may include prescribing various psychotherapeutic techniques. If you happen to be interested in research, you may also explore such questions as the causes of mental disorders or the influence of heredity and environment on personal maladjustment. You may also evaluate new diagnostic and therapeutic procedures.

The setting for your work may be a child guidance center, a correctional institution, a mental hygiene clinic, or a hospital for the mentally retarded or the mentally ill. It may even be a college or university.

COMMUNITY PSYCHOLOGY

The newest field of endeavor for the psychologist is community psychology which, as its name implies, involves the psychologist as an active participant in developing community resources. If you were to choose to work in this area, you would, for instance, serve as a therapeutic resource to individual clients and treatment groups in a specific geographical community.

You might also organize existing community services and multiple levels of professionals and nonprofessionals for the prevention of mental disorders. The newly formed Youth Services Bureaus are a case in point.

Third, you might study psychological and social issues by established methods in the behavioral sciences.

Finally, as a community psychologist you might seek the goal of creating a social environment that offers to its members a sense of "community."

CONSULTING PSYCHOLOGY

Everyone knows what love is, yet everyone seems to have trouble defining it. This same statement might be made regarding consulting psychology. The most inclusive definition seems to this writer to be the following.

"A consulting psychologist is one who has received recognition by his peers as an expert in his area(s) of functioning and who provides technical assistance to individuals and organizations in relation to the psychological dimensions of their work."

The assistance provided by the consulting psychologist is directed to specific work-related problems and is advisory in nature. The consultant has no direct responsibility for its acceptance or implementation.

If you were to choose to work as a consultant, you would first have to become a specialist. Only then could you offer your services, as the consultant does, to other psychologist less knowledgeable in some aspect of their work, or to specialists in other fields who might need assistance in the management of psychological and human relations problems.

You might merely listen to a client's proposed solution to a problem and reflect his view of it. By serving as a mirror, you might help the client review the problem to make sure he is not making a stupid mistake or overlooking a possible solution.

On the other hand, you might serve as a resource person with special knowledge that the client needs to apply to a problem. In such a situation, you might recommend a particular procedure or the use of a particular technological device.

Finally, you might serve as a source of moral support, neither reflecting what the client proposes nor proposing any course of action yourself. By thus expressing confidence in the client, you might help the client to gain the assurance needed by him if he is to proceed.

Quite clearly, your work as a consultant would be defined by your function rather than by your specific area of expertise. Hence, you could specialize in any area of psychology. If the problem would have to do with analysis of data or the design of a study, your particular competence would have to lie in statistics and experimental design. If someone would wish to get help in measuring sensory or perceptual processes, your special knowledge would have to be in sensation and perception. Finally, if someone would come to you with a problem having to do with his relationship with his wife, your specialty would probably be clinical psychology.

EDUCATIONAL PSYCHOLOGY

The educational psychologist investigates processes of mental growth and development. Were you to decide on this area, your job would require you to conduct personal interviews with students. You would administer and score questionnaires and psychological tests of intelligence, achievement, aptitudes and interests.

You would evaluate personal qualifications, using past records, test results, and information derived from your interviews.

You might suggest specific courses and activities with the goal of guiding individuals in their selection of academic or vocational courses leading to suitable careers. Finally, you might develop and apply methods of instructing and training handicapped persons.

The setting in which you would work would usually be the school, although you might also function in a vocational guidance center.

ENGINEERING PSYCHOLOGY

The psychologist working as an engineer is engaged in both basic and applied research. He is a trained scientist whose research products constitute the essential scientific information applied to the problems of a system.

If you were to choose to become an engineering psychologist you would be involved in studying possible procedures for manning a system, operating on the premise that man is an integral part of man-machine systems, just like the hardware, and thus that man's performance must be optimized, just as hardware components, if the system as a whole is to be optimized.

Thus, when an engineering psychologist specifies the layout of a panel or the type of personnel to man a system, he is saying that his specification will give better performance for the system than some other specification. An outstanding example of the kind of work done by the psychologist in this area has been evident in the American space program, wherein both the machines and the men to man them underwent considerable evaluation before any actual trials were run.

ENVIRONMENTAL PSYCHOLOGY

If you are concerned as deeply as many with regard to ecology and the preservation of the world in which we live, you might find environmental psychology of interest to you vocationally.

If you were to enter this area of psychology you would do research on human aspects of environmental problems. You would ask such questions as the following: What are the conditions under which people plan? Under what circumstances are they most likely to take the future into account? What kind of knowledge is most likely to be influential in planning? What is the role of vividness? What is the relative influence of knowledge characterized by imagery? What kind of experience leads to knowledge likely to be acted upon? How important is concreteness? Complexity? Is speed of reaction important? You would probably relate your answers to such concerns of today as population density and mass-produced uniformity.

The setting for your work would probably be the laboratory and the world outside, planning your studies in an office but going out into society to seek your answers.

EXPERIMENTAL PSYCHOLOGY

As its name suggests, this area is enjoyed by the individual who is particularly interested in finding answers to the "why" of human behavior. If you were to choose to be an experimentalist, you would perhaps use mice, guinea pigs, pigeons, dogs, or even monkeys, as well as humans, for your "laboratory animal." Obviously, you could not be a squeamish individual!

After determining what mental or physical characteristic you wished to examine, you would design an experiment for its measurement. Next you would collect, select and refine the data. Then you would arrange the elements into units on a tentative basis. After extensive trials you would standardize the tests or experiments. Finally, you would prepare results with written and pictorial directions for administration, scoring and interpretation. As an example of what you might do, some psychologists are studying how people learn to read so that education in Africa might be advanced as rapidly as possible. They are studying the formal structure of the material to be learned—and how such structures are learned—in hope of improving teaching methods. Another example can be seen in the Head Start program, which uses early education to compensate for social and cultural disadvantages.

As an experimental psychologist, you might seek to change attitudes by presenting people with convincing arguments and facts. Or you might concern yourself with the use of psychology in economics, as for instance in an attempt to find a cure for poverty.

The setting for the work of the experimentalist has long been the laboratory, but quite recently it has been moving out into the social environment in order to gain tools for measurement and to seek out the rules by which the mind works for a certain species in a certain environment.

INDUSTRIAL PSYCHOLOGY

The industrial psychologist applies psychological principles and techniques to industrial problems. If you were to choose this area of psychology for your life work, you would find yourself involved in seeking ways of satisfying both the employer and the employee.

To accomplish your goal, you might have the responsibility of looking into the psychological aspects of personnel procedures, policies and functions in industry to improve the efficiency of the workers. You might also have the task of analyzing jobs to determine the physical and mental requirements necessary for satisfactory job performance.

In addition to applying approved principles of learning to programs for training workers, you might also employ psychological tests and other psychological techniques in the selection, transfer and promotion of workers.

Another of your tasks might be to investigate the causes of employee satisfaction and dissatisfaction, so that you might advise supervisors on the best ways to handle employees.

As a result of these many activities, you might suggest changes in job content, methods of performance, working conditions, and the design of tools and equipment.

The setting in which you would work might be in a college or university, teaching others how to do these various tasks, or conducting research. Most likely, however. you would be employed in an industrial setting, performing administrative services.

PSYCHOMETRICS

As a student you have often encountered psychological measurements. Whenever you have taken a scholastic aptitude or an achievement test, you have been a subject. The tests you took were prepared and scored by a person trained in psychological measurements. Such a person is often known under the job title of "test technician" or "psychometrician."

A person with that title may do a large amount of experimental planning for polls of public opinion. Such polls include prediction of election results (such as the Gallup poll), buying behavior, and attitudes toward almost anyone or anything.

If you were to choose this area of psychology, you would find yourself collecting and organizing data not only for a polling agency but possibly also for a personnel department or a professional group that conducts tests. You would also plan questions to ask in an interview and then actually do the interview. You would probably administer and score psychological tests. If you were to work in a counseling center, that would be your principal job.

You would be happiest in this area if you enjoy working with mathematics and relatively abstract relationships. While you would not have to become an expert in mathematics, you would need to have or to acquire a reasonable facility with numbers. You would also find helpful an appreciation of scientific methods and a natural curiosity about cause and effect relationships in the area of human behavior. Last but not least, if you were to enjoy some of the jobs that might be offered to you, you would need to like to work with people, especially if your job involves interviewing.

The setting for your work might be in one of the large companies where the personnel departments do a great deal of interviewing and testing and thus need the services of people trained in psychological measurement. Other possible settings in which you might work include government research programs, social work agencies, college and university counseling centers, and social science research in universities.

SCHOOL PSYCHOLOGY

School psychology may be classified as a specific branch of educational psychology concerned chiefly with classroom learning. If you were to choose this area in psychology for your vocation, you would have two chief goals: to remove maladaptive behavior in children and to develop a battery of specific assessment procedures that would enhance new learning skills.

You would be aware that your success as a school psychologist would not depend on how many tests you would give or how many reports you would write but rather on the amount of success you would have in reducing maladaptive behavior in the classroom, in accelerating the development of skills, and in helping teachers to become more effective. In your preparation for this work, you would study in order to understand classroom phenomena. Obviously, the setting for your work would be the school.

SOCIAL PSYCHOLOGY

The social psychologist is concerned with psychological aspects of individual and group thought and activity in society. If you were to choose this area of work, you would be involved in developing and altering public attitudes, reactions and behavior.

One of your chief tasks would be to analyze the relation of the individual to various groups: religious, racial, economic or national. You might do this by conducting surveys and polls, using original or standard techniques. With the data thus obtained, you would analyze results to find the reasons for the opinions expressed. You might then suggest programs designed to promote social rapport.

As a social psychologist, you would teach, prepare articles for publication, perform administrative services, or act as a consultant. Most importantly, you would respond to the increasing pressure over the past decade for the psychologist to study phenomena in the field rather than in the laboratory. Thus, you would come down from your ivory tower and immerse yourself in society itself in order to meet its needs and demands.

NEWER AREAS OF PSYCHOLOGY

In addition to the preceding categories of employment, you might want to give some serious attention to the somewhat newer areas of work for the psychologist. The most obvious new sources of employment are in nonuniversity academic settings and independent business and industrial settings. For instance, psychologists are now entering the fields of banking, finance and insurance. Various aspects of the law and the legal profession also seem to be employing psychologists in our society. Probation departments, juvenile courts, and law schools are examples. Last but not least, you might explore the possibility of doing work as a psychologist in independent research centers, state departments of mental health, federal research centers, and the military.

What Factors Affect the Amount of One's Salary?

The amount of salary that you might earn will depend on several factors: the location of your job, the highest degree you hold, your age, the area of psychology in which you might work, and even the fact that you are a female.

With regard to the location of your job, median salaries at all ranks tend to be higher in the northeast region of the United States. One must bear in mind, however, that expenses might also be higher there. Salaries in the West tend to be somewhat lower at all ranks.

Do Salaries Differ Significantly If One Has Only the Master's Degree Rather Than the Doctorate?

If you compare the income of psychologists holding the doctorate with those holding only the master's degree, you will find some significant differences, as you can see in the chart below.

TABLE 8-I.

| | Ph.D. | | Master's degree | |
	1968	1970	1968	1970
Self-employed	23,000	25,000	—	—
Private industry	19,000	22,500	14,500	17,000
Federal government	15,800	18,400	14,000	14,700
State and local government	15,800	18,400	11,000	12,100
Nonprofit organizations	15,000	17,000	10,800	12,150
Educational institutions				
Calendar year	15,000	16,500	12,000	14,000
Academic year	12,000	13,200	10,500	12,000

Quite clearly, the Ph.D. commands a higher income than the master's degree. This differential also shows up when one goes back to 1960 for a comparison. The average salary at that time was $9,000 for the doctorate and $7,000 for the master's (a difference of $2,000). Ten years later, in 1970, those salaries had risen to $16,000 for the doctorate and $13,100 for the master's degree (a difference of $2,900).

Also worth noting is the fact that the young person thirty to thirty-four years of age, with the benefit of a competitive situation in the field of psychology, earned $8,000 in 1960, a thousand dollars more than the psychologist with a master's degree, and $13,000 in 1970, only a hundred dollars less than the master's degree psychologist.

Income also increased with age, to the age of forty, after which it tended to plateau, remaining relatively level throughout the entire range. Income also increased with number of years since the doctorate, until fifteen to twenty years after receipt of the degree, after which it also tended to plateau.

Do Salaries Vary Depending on the Area of Psychology That One Chooses for One's Vocation?

If you examine the chart just above, you will note that the psychologists with the Ph.D. who are self-employed earn the largest income. (If you will recall, the psychologist holding only a master's degree is barred from private practice.) The next highest income is earned, in both groups, by those working in private industry. However, master's degree psychologists have median salaries that are $5,500 less than those earned by psychologists holding doctorates. Academic psychologists obviously receive the lowest salaries.

The chart also points up the fact that salaries differ depending upon the tasks one performs. Quite clearly managerial tasks and the roles of a consultant provide the greatest remuneration, while teaching in a university setting is valued least, if one were to judge on the basis of the salaries paid. One must note, however, that the professor has access to many fringe benefits. For instance, faculty children and sometimes spouses may be granted free tuition. The professor herself may have opportunities for extra work, moonlighting, or summer school, the latter two sometimes amounting to 10 to 20 per cent of her basic salary.

Whether one is male or female also makes a difference when salaries are being considered. Many employers still apply different hiring, training and promotion policies to women workers. As a consequence, males earn substantially more overall than do the females.

If you consider university psychology departments as an example, only 9 percent of the women, compared to 29 percent of the men, earn $17,000 or more for the academic year, while 30 percent of the women and only 10 percent of the men earn salaries as low as $10,000 or less. In spite of their lower pay, the women psychologists spend more time in teaching than do the men, 19 percent of the women teaching at least eleven hours a week compared to only 7 percent of the men. In other words, their rate of pay is even smaller than indicated above. In addition, more of the men psychologists teach only graduate students (29% compared to 24% of the women) and more of the women (29% compared to 11% of the men) teach only undergraduate courses.

Even when women hold doctorates and have earned them from top-rated universities or have published as much as the men, they are still paid lower salaries than the men and receive less recognition in the form of high rank and tenure.

Will a Woman Psychologist Experience Any Other Form of Discrimination?

Yes. This has always been true historically. Not too long ago women were considered as second class citizens, unable to vote or hold office. Laws even made married women and their property subject to the direct and almost unlimited control of their husbands. Even today, whether men are willing to admit the fact or not, they are still discriminating, albeit in more subtle ways, against the female sex.

The double bind is an example. If you smile innocently at a male in the office, he may interpret this as evidence of some devious motive. On the other hand, if you don't smile, then you are aloof, basically withdrawn, and lacking in femininity.

Similarly, the length of your skirt may be interpreted in two different ways. If you wear your skirts short, you are said to be trying to arouse every man near enough to observe. On the other hand, if you wear your skirts long, you are accused of being afraid of men and, what is more, you are said to have become a professional as a defense, the reason of course for your perceived hostility.

A third double bind is malleability. If you are flexible in your views, you must lack firm convictions, but if you are "not amenable to suggestion" then you are clearly (f)rigid, which "everyone knows" is true of the female professional.

Still another double bind occurs with regard to your job performance. If you accomplish too much, you are ambitious. If you do too little, you are incompetent.

If you do get a job, when the budget is cut you are the first to go. Your boss may seek ample justification for his action, but you know the real reason why.

While you will experience discrimination in most areas of psychology, you will find it greatest in industrial psychology. This area is so male dominated at present and women constitute such a small percentage of the membership that women have not yet been able to acquire much, if any, status in the profession. In fact, the preponderance of men at any professional gathering of industrial psychologist is so common an occurrence that the one or two women present could very easily ask themselves if the existence of the woman industrial psychologist is real or just an illusion. This concern is underlined by the fact that all of the myths that keep the woman executive out of the top-level conference meetings also serve to keep the woman psychologist from being able to study and work with upper-level management.

As an example of the fact that women are in the minority in this field, only eight women are Fellows in the Division of Industrial Psychology compared to 248 men; only twenty-nine women are members compared to 748 men; and only twelve women are associates out of 165 men. Moreover, the female members are somewhat older than their male counterparts, a slightly smaller percentage have the Ph.D., and of those with their doctorates, the women received theirs a few years later in life.

Yet, if you are determined to make this area your vocational goal, you should choose as your electives in college some courses in commerce and accounting, which you will find of great advantage in helping the personnel manager give consideration to your abilities. This is particularly true since, even for men, the acceptance of a psychologist in industry is still slight because of the preference for the use of consultants. You will also have to gird yourself to accept a smaller salary than a man with comparable skills. Women just earn much less than the men. According to a recent study, the average woman earned $10,175 less than her male counterpart, the average 1969 income for men being $25,523 compared to $15,348 for women. Clearly, equal opportunity and equal pay for equal work do not exist for women in this area of psychology.

Is the Situation Complicated If You Are
Not Only a Woman But Married?

It is indeed! As a married professional woman, you will encounter even more barriers in your pursuit of your professional goals. (I can state this definitely from my own experience!) Thus, your commitment must be even greater than that of the male if you are to counteract the negative atmosphere you will encounter.

One way in which you may strengthen yourself as you "go forth to battle" is to read the literature on career women in which you can find example after example of individuals who have tenaciously pursued their occupational goals while also taking care of their family responsibilities.

There is usually nothing derogatory in the question "How did you get into this field?" when asked of a man, but when asked of a woman—and particularly of a married woman—it frequently implies that she is "deviant" is some way. Moreover, your own sincerity and commitment will be questioned implicitly or explicitly every time you wish to change your job or seek advancement.

To keep up your morale, you must be aware that many married professional women have succeeded better than men even when judged by male criteria. For example, one criterion for judging an academic psychologist is the amount published. Married women Ph.D.'s holding full-time positions published more, on the average, than either men or single women. This finding contradicts the belief that women are more devoted to their home and family than to their jobs. It also suggests that women in general are more, rather than less, productive than men.

What About the Future Prospects in Psychology?

Looking into the future, forecasters predict that salaries in the future will fall and that the supply of psychologists will diminish. Unless there should be nonacademic shifts in demand, the market for psychologists is expected to diminish considerably in the late 1970s and early 1980s. Thus, you will want to recognize the fact that you will have to get better grades and do better work than your male colleagues if you are to hold on to your job and succeed in the field of psychology.

Still think you want to be a psychologist? Good luck to you!

CHAPTER 9

TEACHING IN SECONDARY AND ELEMENTARY SCHOOLS

GWENDOLYN H. AUSTIN AND PRESTON M. ROYSTER

Introduction
Job Description
Job Requirements
Salary and Other Benefits
Job Opportunities
Job Permanency
Displacement of Black Educators and Students
Multicultural Challenges
Teacher Supply and Demand
Women in Education
Conclusion

//

INTRODUCTION

CAREER CHOICES IN AMERICA have often caused great anxiety and frequently even frustration on the part of many black Americans, for until recently only a few career doors were open to them. The profession of teaching, however, has been a major choice of black Americans for a variety of reasons. First, because of segregated school systems, the existence of the black school meant that teachers would have to be selected from among blacks; therefore, young people chose teaching because it seemed a practical area when considering the totality of the American society.

A second reason for this choice was the socio-political realities which prevailed at that time. Political decision-making rested in the hands of white people who all too often limited the career options for blacks.

A third reason was that black people had come to realize that education was the major vehicle for changing the economic and social plight of black Americans, and many sought to educate their younger black brothers and sisters through the profession of teaching as a career choice.

A fourth reason was the status and security accorded to teachers in black communities. To blacks, the holding of a high status job which was safe from white incursion was an ultimate attainment.

Not to be overlooked as another important reason was the desire to become a learned individual and to share that motivation with others. Many blacks elected to teach as a demonstration of that strong motivation.

When viewing developments of the 1960's with the effects of major legislation, major social changes, and the opening up of career opportunities previously denied blacks, one may wonder if black Americans should still consider teaching as a career choice.

In order to help the reader make a more intelligent decision, we shall further explore teaching as a career choice for blacks.

JOB DESCRIPTION

According to the National Education Association estimates, there were 1,122,103 elementary school and 978,199 secondary school classroom teachers, making a total of 2,100,302 teachers serving 47,707,628 children in 17,036 school districts during the 1972-73 school year.[1]

Editors Note: This chapter also appears in CAREER GUIDANCE FOR BLACK ADOLESCENTS: A GUIDE TO SELECTED OCCUPATIONS published by Charles C Thomas, Publisher, Springfield, Illinois. Due to the great similarity in vocational discrimination experienced by both blacks and women, we felt this chapter very naturally fit into this book.

[1]National Education Association, *"Estimates of School Statistics, 1972-73,"* Research *Report 1972-R 12* (Washington, D.C., National Education Association, 1973), pp. 6-12.

Local school districts throughout the United States differ greatly in organizational structure, character and size. A local school district may range from a one-room, one-teacher rural system to a large urban system serving thousands of children.

The role of the teacher may vary greatly according to the school district, as well as from school to school within a given school district. In some schools, teachers conduct only large group instruction, and all teachers must follow a set curriculum.

In still other schools, teachers individualize instruction and are free to innovate.

Over the last five years an approach termed "open education" has emerged. In open education, the teacher leaves the center of the stage, so to speak, and becomes a facilitator of learning; the student becomes the center of attraction wherein his individual needs are considered and he is offered a wide range and variety of options in regard to his activities. The concept of open education may be implemented in any type of physical plant whether it be open space or a one-room school building.

Local teacher unions, along with the National Education Association, are becoming actively involved in some areas and are helping dictate job descriptions and working conditions.

Superintendents, school boards, principals, communities, state education agencies, and numerous other groups or individuals are all involved in determining the role and working conditions for a teacher.

JOB REQUIREMENTS

The completion of a bachelor's degree with an emphasis on teacher education is widely accepted as the minimum requirement for becoming an effective teacher. There is an increasing trend, however, toward the completion of a master's degree as the minimal level of acceptance for persons regarded as fully qualified teachers. Another trend indicates a higher proportion of secondary teachers than previously recorded has completed the master's degree or higher.[2]

[2]*National Education Association, "Teachers Supply and Demand in Public Schools," 1972," Research Report 1972-RB* (Washington, D.C., National Education Association, 1972), p. 46.

There are some states, however, that reported for the school year 1971-72 that more than 10 percent of their elementary teachers were without the bachelor's degree.[3]

Possession of degrees alone, however, does not necessarily make one an effective teacher. To be effective one must be interested in teaching. He must be dedicated to teaching. He must have respect for the children he teaches. He must have pride in his profession. He must be humane and understanding. He must be able to relate effectively to parents and the broad community. In addition, he must be capable of facilitating the child's learning.

Teaching is a demanding career—one which requires an examination of one's being, one's entire thought patterns, and one's basic ideas about people, life and things. It is a career which demands the highest levels of creativity and imagination known to mankind. It requires improvision in the most difficult learning situations, and it requires massive understanding of the society's mores, customs, practices and policies. In this decade, the teacher must understand changes in every facet of American life and its cultures which include many different styles of learning. Teaching requires the kind of individual who can effect the kind of modifications necessary to make a positive difference in the lifestyle of young people.

Dr. James Boyer, assistant professor of Curriculum and Instruction at Kansas State University, in discussing the human dimensions of urban teaching, stated the job requirements quite succinctly when he said,

> A teaching certificate usually indicates or implies that its holder has command of a body of data (knowledge). The real test of a teacher, however, comes when he or she can demonstrate the ability to utilize that data humanistically in helping urban learners reach goals commensurate with survival in the great urban centers of our country.[4]

There is a need for black teachers dedicated to and capable of

---

[3]*National Education Association, "Teachers Supply and Demand in Public Schools, 1972," Research Report 1972-R8* (Washington, D.C., National Education Association, 1972), p. 46.

[4]James B. Boyer and Warren L. Paul, *The Bulletin of the Bureau of School Service,* The University of Kentucky—"Urban Education" Issue Volume XLV, Number 4, 1973, Pages 5-8.

helping their black brothers and sisters gain the insights, knowledge, and survival skills necessary to cope with their social and economic plights. As long as negative white attitudes, black ghettos, and black rural poverty-stricken areas exist, teachers must be able to make the black children educationally prepared to stand up and take their rightful places in society.

SALARY AND OTHER BENEFITS

For 1972-73, the average salary of classroom teachers was estimated at $10,114. The estimated average salary of elementary schoolteachers was $9,823 while that of secondary schoolteachers was $10,460.[5]

The average salaries among states differ greatly, however, and salaries in some states may fall far below the average. In fact, it was estimated that in 1972-73, 16.4 percent of the classroom teachers would be paid less than $7,500.[6]

Although the teaching profession may not be the most lucrative one, it can be one of the most rewarding.

The rewards may come in a variety of ways. It may be that kiss you received from that tall, handsome, distinguished-looking young man who approached you in the airport and whom you recognized as the short, devilish little fellow you taught some years ago.

It may be the picture you received from that Air Force Academy cadet and the note that read, "To the kindest and most wonderful teacher a person could ever have."

It could have been that college graduation invitation you received from that black brother whom you helped when others had indicated he was not college material.

These and countless other rewards help make the teaching profession self-fulfilling.

JOB OPPORTUNITIES

People in all professions have a continual desire to be properly recognized, rewarded and promoted to the more rewarding and

[5]National Education Association, *"Estimates of School Statistics, 1972-1973," Research Report 1972-R 12* (Washington, D.C., National Education Association, 1973), p. 14.
[6]Ibid, p. 13.

prestigous jobs in their professions. Teachers and others in the education profession have this desire also.

For the first time in American history, there is a nationwide search for black teachers and administrators. This is true for school districts in the North and West that have neither hired black teachers in the past nor have ever had adequate or significant numbers of such educators. This means that districts having small numbers of black citizens, or none at all, are seeking black educators. It is also true for districts that have populations of white, Chicano, Oriental, Indian and other cultural backgrounds.

It might be worthwhile to discuss the reasons these options now exist. (1) It could be that white society is making a drastic and radical determination to make America a true "melting pot." But, there is little evidence to suggest that this is true. (2) It could be that America, as a whole, has become a law abiding society, a thought which is refuted by violations of the court rulings cited on page 9. (3) It could be that there is a desire to cope with the cross-cultural and ethnic issues, and make a "multicultural society"* a reality.

The average observer of the educational scene, to be more specific, will readily note that the above trend creates more teaching opportunities for black educators than ever existed in America's past. It should be added that this trend is applied equally in its demand and search for teachers from other minority groups.

In spite of federal and other demands for black educators, there is little evidence to suggest that the white supremist attitudes have adequately accepted the idea of equal opportunity sufficiently to open administrative positions in adequate numbers, to black and other minority educators. Dr. Benjamin Epstein, Chairman, Status and Welfare Committee National Association of Secondary School Principals in his testimony before the Select Committee of Equal Educational Opportunity said,

> When schools are desegregated and must serve black and white students alike, the powers that be who select the staff for these schools apparently try to make sure that white students and teachers will not

---

*A societal condition in which individuals of varied racial and ethnic groups intermingle socially, professionally and philosophically.

be under the authority of black principals.[7]

Dr. Epstein also stated that, "there seems to be little or no compunction about having the situation in reverse—black children and teachers under the authority of white principals . . . a pattern so traditional that it dare not be altered."[8] Even though the above is true and massive displacement in desegregating southern schools exists, nationally, the number of black superintendents, assistant superintendents and other "front office administrators" is larger than ever before.

JOB PERMANENCY

Job security, which allows one the freedom of mind to concentrate on performance, is sought by people in all lines of work. More black citizens are found in the teaching profession, both in public schools and in institutions of higher education, than in any other profession requiring a college degree. This is probably true because historically, employment opportunities for black citizens have been extremely limited in the private sector. It is also true, perhaps, because white Americans have insisted on unrealistic education credentials for black employees. Consequently, the black population has established a strong cleavage to education as the single best way to establish and project black capability, security, self-confidence and esteem. Also, because of previous and current racial separatist practices in education, the teaching profession has demanded a sizeable number of black educators. This condition exists in most states from the West Coast to the East Coast with a significantly larger concentration of black teachers in the southern and border states because of the great concentration of black citizens and previously all black schools in these states.

Because of other factors which inherently emanate from the above conditions, teaching has provided, with several exceptions to be explored later, a great degree of employment security and permanency for black teachers. One of the reasons is that state

[7]Dr. Benjamin Epstein, Chairman, Status and Welfare Committee, National Association of Secondary School Principals, before the Select Committee on Equal Education Opportunity, U.S. Senate, June 14, 1971, pp. 11.
[8]Ibid.

credential systems and tenure systems that cover black and white teachers are uniform. Additionally, this mass of black teachers provided the black leadership, and to some extent, power (even though it proved to be rather weak with the threat of having blacks teach and supervise whites) that sustained black teachers.

Job permanency for black teachers is further enhanced by a December 1, 1969, Federal Court ruling (Singleton vs. Jackson [Mississippi]). Municipal Separate School District which requires the use of "objective and reasonably nondiscriminatory standards from among all staff of the school district" when a reduction in force is required in a desegregating school. The security of teaching jobs for black teachers is somewhat insured by a June, 1971, Supreme Court ruling which states that "employees of Mississippi (Columbia, Mississippi, school district) cannot screen Negroes from jobs with tests (National Teacher Examination) that do not measure their qualifications."

DISPLACEMENT OF BLACK EDUCATORS AND STUDENTS

Public school desegregation, particularly in the South, has brought widespread maltreatment of black educators and students. The demands for school desegregation resulted in scores of black teachers being displaced from their teaching and administrative positions thus causing an economic disaster for many black Americans who chose teaching. Recent National Education Association figures show that as many as 32,000 black teachers may have been displaced and hundreds of others are now in desegregated schools but have been demoted.[9]

For black southern educators, the desegregation of schools resulted in dismissal, demotion and displacement. The pattern in the southern states has been to (1) dismiss black administrators and educators both at the time of desegregation, and continuing thereafter, for little or no provocation or (2) demote all or most black administrators, supervisors, coaches, bandleaders, counselors and others in positions of leadership and (3) fill excessive numbers of vacancies with white replacements as positions are created or vacated. In the northern and western states the practice—years

[9]Phi Delta Kappan, Volume LV, Number 1, September 1973, pp. 85-86.

of failing to hire adequate numbers of black and other minority educators in leadership positions—is similar. As previously mentioned, most northern and western states had few black educators until recent years. Consequently, the "'last hired, first fired" practice has caused disproportionate displacement of Black educators when enrollments and budgets have decreased.[10]

The problems confronting black students in desegregating southern schools are equally as devastating. Data reported by Dr. Epstein of the National Association of Secondary School Principals indicate that far fewer black students are being graduated from integrated southern schools than were graduated in segregated schools in those same states. The reasons were found to be that unequal treatment of black and white students is widespread.[11] Observable differences in treatment are: (1) blacks are most often expelled or suspended when a situation develops between a black and a white student; (2) rules are being established which require expulsion after a certain number of offenses (offenses committed by the white student are seldom recorded but most, or all, are recorded for the black student, thus more expulsions) ; and (3) black students are forced out by general harassment and by displacement in special education and general curricular. Ironically, the same situation prevails in the northern and western schools where black and other minority students are involved. The main difference is that the disguise of friendliness and concern are substituted for the southern display of hostility and bigotry.

According to Dr. Paul A. Miller, former president of the American Association of School Administrators, the American Association of School Administrators considers these practices a national disgrace. He stated that the association fully supports the spirit and letter of federal statutes which require equal employment opportunity for black and other minority educators and equal educational opportunity for black and other minority students. The National Education Association appears to have taken

---

[10]Noel P. Fox, "Teacher Unemployment in Michigan Continues to Rise," (Unpublished issue paper presented as testimony before Judge Fox, Michigan, 1971), p. 18.

a similarly strong stand against unfair treatment of black educators and students in desegregated schools.

MULTICULTURAL CHALLENGES

The newly integrated or desegregated society in which black teachers are sought and likely placed in all white classes or classes with sizeable numbers of persons from other social groups demands that all teachers, but particularly black ones, have experiences and skills that allow them to work successfully with other racial groups. This means that black education students, traditionally from the rural areas, with their newly acquired racial identities must use every possible opportunity to gain understanding and experiences with the majority society. At first glance this may appear to suggest that black teachers amalgamate and compromise their blackness. Nothing could be further from the truth. On second thought, this ability tends to reflect the adequacy and indeed possibly the superiority of black teachers, for the white majority group has continually failed to effectively and positively relate to and understand racial and ethnic groups other than itself. This factor might very well mean success for black and other minority educators while spelling failure for white ones. One only needs to look at California, for example, where large numbers of black, white, Chicano and Oriental populations exist to assess the importance of being able to relate to and teach children of different cultures and languages.

If we are going to meet these multicultural challenges, it seems appropriate to advise that black students use their summer work experiences, and periodic travels to broaden their understandings in these complex and sensitive areas.

Becoming adequate in these areas will provide greater assurances of success in the all-important areas of dealing with and helping to overcome the prejudices and stereotypes of parents, students, co-workers and supervisors. Even though there is a great demand for black teachers, the degree to which they are successful still depends as strongly on resourcefulness and knowledge of subject area.

TEACHER SUPPLY AND DEMAND

People are constantly asking whether or not there is an over-supply of teachers. The following estimates for 1972-73 were reported by the National Education Association.

At the beginning of the 1972-73 school year there were 102,852 elementary teacher education graduates and 126,438 secondary teacher education graduates available for employment; however, 51,800 beginning teachers in elementary schools and 80,300 beginning teachers in secondary schools were employed.[12]

These figures seem to indicate an oversupply. When one considers individual disciplines, however, there is still a shortage in math and in trade-industrial-vocational-technical subjects.

There is a limited supply compared with demand in the natural and physical sciences and in industrial arts. The supply is just about equal to demand in special education and in distributive education.

Another category in which there is a shortage of teachers relates purely to race. School systems throughout the country are now in the business of seeking black teachers. This seems to be related to two positive societal changes. One of them is that many white leaders have demonstrated more willingness to provide equal employment opportunity for all citizens. Another one seems to be based on the widespread impact of the Civil Rights Act of 1964, school desegregation rulings by the U.S. Supreme Court, and numerous rulings by federal circuit courts.

Some of the areas most frequently reported as having an oversupply of qualified applicants were social studies, health and physical education, English language arts, elementary school teaching, and foreign language.

WOMEN IN EDUCATION

Traditionally, education has been a woman's field; however, over the last twenty years, more and more men have entered the profession. In 1940, 22 percent of the nation's teachers were men.

[12]*National Education Association, "Teacher Supply and Demand in Public Schools, 1972," Research Report 1972-R8* (Washington, D.C.), National Education Association, 1972), p. 21.

By 1968, there were 31 percent male teachers in the country. According to National Education Association statistics, men seem to be concentrated at the high school level where they comprise 54 percent of the high school teachers. Women still, however, dominate the elementary teaching scene, accounting for approximately 85 percent of the elementary teaching force.

Regardless of the predominance of women in the teaching profession as a whole, women are vanishing from the administrative leadership of American public schools. For example, although 85 percent of the elementary teachers are women, 80 percent of the principals are men.

On the secondary level, of nearly 16,000 senior high school principals in America, only 222 or 1.4 percent are women.[13]

This pattern of unequal advancement into administrative positions can most assuredly be viewed as sex discrimination.

Nevertheless, the entering of male into the teaching profession itself should indeed be lauded and encouraged, for many of our black and white children who come from broken or fatherless homes need very desperately a male image.

CONCLUSION

We have presented a number of extremely negative conditions that continue to exist for black teachers and which may lead one to become somewhat reluctant to choose teaching as a career. These facts have not been presented to drive one from teaching but rather to enable those interested in education to gain a better understanding of the situation and to be better prepared to become a successful teacher.

Yes, black Americans should consider teaching as a career. Black Americans have a history of teaching and learning under the most difficult circumstances, but in spite of this they have developed creativity and have become highly educated regardless of national efforts at times to keep them from learning. Further, the necessity for teaching others has prompted black America to de-

---

[13]Andrew Barnes, "Women Lose Power in Public Schools," *Washington Post* (September 22, 1973) p. 1.

velop superb ability to improvise. It is no secret that segregated schools, especially those populated by black children, were often underequipped, undersupplied, and understaffed. Despite this case, black Americans devised systems of delivering quality instructional services to children. Black America's history is replete with individuals who are products of schools which were poorly equipped with poorly paid teachers in social systems which severely limited the broader educational opportunities open to others. So why should black Americans continue to choose teaching? First, because the art and science of teaching is still one of America's most significant careers. We could not continue to be a democratic nation were it not for the efforts of teachers. Black Americans can deliver that service and should enjoy the feelings of accomplishment which characterize teaching when it is well done.

A second reason that blacks should consider teaching as a career is that their history places them in a unique position to assist this country in the transition from an essentially monoracial, monocultural school program to a diversified, multi-ethnic program of instruction.

A third reason that black Americans should choose teaching as a career is that children need the dedication, the determination, the tenacity of those black young people who recognize that values are imbedded in the style of teaching and in the multifaceted roles of the teacher's task. In other words, diversity in the learning process is so amply exhibited by talented and alert black teachers that the young white child who has an early experience with a black teacher could be considered experientially more adapt than the child not having had the cross-culture experience. He learns much more than cognitive data, and he learns that one's racial identification does not automatically make him superior or inferior. This is a lesson which many Americans still have not learned. The innovative black teacher can deliver that lesson.

Finally, black Americans should choose teaching as a career because we have now reached a point where we can be selective about who serves as a teacher in our schools. The production of average teachers has been tremendous, and no longer is there a cry for "anyone who will consider teaching for employment."

Now schools can be much more selective and should use that opportunity to employ only the most capable, most human, most creative persons available to deliver instructional services in a desegregated society. How those decisions are reached will still make a difference in the perceptions held by those who assign teachers, but *some of those most capable are also black.*

While teachers still have preferences about the children they are assigned to teach, no professional teacher can ever expect to have classes that are not desegregated for an entire teaching career. Those who offer their services as teachers must expect to work with children who happen to be racially or ethnically different from the teacher. That creates a new dimension in human relations, but "teachers for the real world" already know that human relations are more important than traditional data banks in the form of credentials. Therefore, black America must continue to consider teaching as a career choice because the plight of black Americans demanded that they be super-conscious of human beings. Sheer survival as a human being meant being acutely aware of people and since this had to be a part of black America's lifestyle, why shouldn't it be utilized today in the delivery of more effective instructional services to all children?

If America is to ever rid itself of the myth of the "melting pot," the black teacher will have to be the new consciousness of curricular and human diversity in order to improve the self image of minority children. A recent article on diversified curriculum stated,

> Children must be taught through a desegregated, diversified curriculum that differences are to be appreciated rather than challenged. Inclusion of minorities (of all descriptions) into the curricular program helps to bring about that appreciation. Historically, writers and publishers have excluded the records and accomplishments of outstanding blacks, Mexican Americans, and other minorities whose contributions helped to shape America and to make it the great nation our schools teach that it is. This exclusion has left the white learners (as well as some minority learners) feeling that minorities are not to be appreciated and respected, since these reactions are usually in accordance with recognized contributions.[14]

---

[14]James B. Boyer, "Desegregating The Curriculum," *Educational Leadership,* Volume 30, Number 8, ASCD, NEA, (May, 1973) pp. 759, 760.

Our country cannot afford to lose the compassion, the creativity, the innovative minds of professional teachers who happen to be black. Choose on!

CHAPTER 10

SEX DISCRIMINATION IN EDUCATION: AN OVERVIEW*

Early Education Reinforces Ideas of Male Superiority
Sex Discrimination in Secondary Education
Biases in Postsecondary Education
Women with Special Needs Encounter Additional Difficulties
The Education System as an Employer
Research and Development: Help or Hindrance?

A S THE DECADE ADVANCES, equality for women is emerging as one of education's thorniest and most urgent issues. And little wonder.

At a time when women are demanding equality as both a human and a constitutional right, our schools are still imparting concepts of male superiority. Although women are close to half the working population, education is still primarily preparing them to be housewives. As an employer, the educational system is equally guilty. Women working in education can generally expect lower pay, less responsibility, and far less chance for advancement than men working at the same level.

The situation is not without its bright spots. But mounting evidence makes it clear that unequal treatment of the sexes is the rule in education, not the exception. As a girl progresses through

*Part I of *A Look at Women in Education: Issues and Answers for HEW*—Report of the Commissioner's Task Force on the Impact of Office of Education Programs on Women.

the education system, she confronts serious biases and restrictions at each level simply because she is female.

EARLY EDUCATION REINFORCES IDEAS OF MALE SUPERIORITY

From the time they first start school, children learn from teachers, textbooks, games and films that males are superior to females.

Elementary school textbooks reveal startling biases. Females are continually underplayed as topics of interest. An extensive study covering 144 readers from fifteen reading series, varying from primer to sixth grade level, disclosed that while boys were the focus of 881 "amusing and exciting" stories, only 344 of these stories centered around girls. Similarly, there were 282 stories featuring adult males, but only 127 stories about women. In addition, there were 131 biographies of famous men, but only twenty-three of famous women.[1]

Derogatory comments aimed at girls in general were common in all these readers. One reader depicts a girl's getting lost in London with the caption, "Girls are always late." Another primer denigrates girls with a "Look at her, Mother, just look at her. She is just like a girl. She gives up." and again with "You cannot write and spell well enough to write a book. You are just two little girls."[2]

Other sex stereotypes are commonly threaded through grade school curriculum materials. Girls emerge as passive, dependent and incompetent, while boys are active, self-reliant and successful. Mothers mostly appear as housecleaners, clothesmenders, grocery shoppers and cake bakers; fathers are wage earners.

The negative influence that biased curriculum materials exert on children is reinforced by differences in the way teachers and administrators treat boys and girls. Teachers communicate their expectations of "feminine" and "masculine" behavior in subtle ways: girls are asked to do light classroom chores (watering the flowers or decorating the Valentine box), boys are assigned to the heavier and more responsible tasks (moving chairs or hall patrol). Physically active girls are labeled "tomboys"; boys who cry are "sissies."

Then too, the traditional classroom setup, with children sitting quietly row by row, is difficult for most children, but especially hard for boys who have been encouraged from birth to be physically active. Teachers tend to reward passivity and obedience, qualities many girls have already acquired.

This dichotomy in roles is undoubtedly reinforced when children look at adult roles in their own schools, where they are likely to see that women teach and men run things: an early and potentially damaging lesson in "career education." For while 85 percent of all public school elementary teachers are women, 79 percent of the elementary school principals are men.[3]

By the time children are ready to leave grade school, they have already begun to develop distinct impressions of the limitations placed on them because of their sex.

SEX DISCRIMINATION IN SECONDARY EDUCATION

Once children reach secondary school, they are likely to confront even more rigid sex stereotyping. Both girls and boys may be prevented from taking advantage of certain educational activities, although restrictions facing girls are far more serious than those boys usually face.

Sex-biased Curriculum Materials

Sex biases in the curriculum are a problem at this level, too, though the focus has shifted: women are ignored more often than maligned. In history and social studies texts, for example, women —their achievements and their concerns—are virtually invisible. The history of women's exploitation and their struggle for equality is dealt with superficially, if mentioned at all.

Stereotyping Interests and Abilities

Early on, girls and boys discover they are expected to develop different "aptitudes": boys in math and science, girls in English and the arts. Teachers, principals and parents may encourage boys to pursue these "masculine" fields, but admonish girls to stick to the "feminine" fields. There is no question that these sex stereotypes have an effect. The National Assessment Study dis-

covered, for instance, that while there was little difference between boys and girls in science writing at age nine, the gap
widened increasingly at ages thirteen, seventeen, and young adulthood.[4]

Sex-Segregated Courses

Children who do display unconventional interests may be
blocked from pursuing them because appropriate courses are restricted to the other sex. Home economics and industrial arts
classes are frequently segregated by sex, making it difficult for
both sexes to acquire basic home management skills. Men don't
learn to cook or mend; women can't put up a shelf or fix an
electrical outlet. Young people are becoming interested in what
the other half is learning: in an informal survey taken in Boston
recently, girls in traditionally female vocational education said
they would rather take industrial arts than home economics, if
they had the chance. Students of both sexes have begun to demand
that these courses be coeducational. A few pioneering school
districts have combined home economics and industrial arts into
courses covering a range of "survival" skills, others have devised
"bachelor cooking" courses, while others have simply opened up
the old courses to both sexes.

Segregated Academic and Vocational Schools:
Separate But Not Equal

Opportunities for girls are further limited by restricted admissions in schools. Academic and vocational high schools in large
school districts sometimes exclude one sex entirely or require
higher admissions standards for girls than for boys. Simply because of their sex, students may find themselves ineligible for the
school offering the best or only courses in their field of interest.

Until recently, New York City excluded girls from two of the
city's high-quality public academic high schools specializing in
science, mathematics and technology. Two years after a court
order opened the first school, the board of education was still
listing these schools for "boys only" in its official catalogue.[5]

Vocational high schools in big cities are also frequently sex
segregated. A 1971 telephone survey by the Office of Education's

Office of Legislation found, for example, that the District of Columbia had four (two for men, two for women) ; Baltimore, four (also two for each) ; and New York City, eighteen (thirteen for males, five for females) .

Separate does not mean equal. Boys' vocational high schools tend to offer training for more diverse and better paying jobs. The segregated schools in New York City prevent girls from taking courses in seventeen different vocational fields: architectural drafting, dental labs processing, jewelry making, industrial chemistry and upholstery as well as areas in heavy industry. Boys are excluded from two.[6]

A comparison of Boston's two trade high schools, one for each sex, is particularly revealing.

Boys at Boston Trade High choose from courses in automobile mechanics, basic electronics, cabinetmaking, carpentry, drafting, electrical technology, machine shop, painting, plumbing, printing, sheet metal and welding. At Trade High School for Girls, on the other hand, students are only offered programs in clothing, foods, beauty culture, and commercial art. The average expected wage for trades taught at Trade High School for Girls is 47 percent less than that for the trades available at Boston Trade High School for Boys.[7]

In addition, nonvocational course offerings at these schools are determined by sex. At Trade High School for Girls, students take typing and merchandising, while boys at Boston Trade learn geometry, trigonometry and physics. Girls can study biology but not chemistry. Interestingly, the Boston school system makes exceptions for boys who want to be admitted to the girls' trade school (seven were enrolled in 1970) , but no exceptions have ever been made for girls who sought admission to the trade school for boys.[8]

Limitations in Vocational Education

Justifications for this kind of rank discrimination range from the well-meaning ("She won't be able to get a job") to the absurd ("We can't let girls do metal work because they have to wear masks and work with sparks.") [9] Whatever the excuse, schools must stop denying students free choice in vocational training.

The fact is that some women want training in vocations now dominated by men, and vice versa. Women have succeeded, despite tremendous resistance, in all of these fields; during World War II the popular "Rosie the Riveter" served as evidence that women were effectively replacing men in many industry jobs. Sex discrimination in employment has been illegal since 1964; now it is illegal in vocational schools, too.

Equality in job training is not a minor concern for women. Despite the persistent myth that "woman's place is in the home," women are now a permanent and growing sector of the work force. Within the past thirty years, the number of women in the work force has more than doubled, so that today two out of every five workers are women.[10] Nearly two thirds of the new jobs created during the 1960's were held by women.[11]

Nor are women only temporarily employed or merely working for "pin money." Seventy per cent of all women employed are working full-time, and the average woman worker has a full-time worklife expectancy of twenty-five years.[12] Nearly half the women employed in 1971 were working because of pressing economic need.[13]

So long as the schools continue to steer girls into vocational training for low-paying jobs, they will continue to contribute to the earnings gap between working women and working men. That gap is substantial and growing worse. In 1955, a woman working full-time earned only 64 percent of a man's earnings, but by 1970, she was only earning 59 percent as much.[14]

Athletics

Schools sponsor physical education and extramural sports because educators recognize the importance of life-long habits of physical fitness. These habits are needed as much by women, as workers and mothers, as by men. However, girls get short shrift in physical education, both at the secondary and higher education levels. Schools and colleges devote greater resources to boys' than to girls' athletics: in facilities, coaches, equipment and interscholastic competition. In one midwestern district, school officials spent ten times as much on boys' athletics as on girls' and there is no reason to believe that this school district was unusual.[15] Girls are often either excluded from interscholastic competition or required to play under restrictive rules especially designed for girls' games. In one case, state rules for high school athletics forced a high school to deny its best tennis player both coaching and the chance to compete. Why? The athlete was female.[16]

Expelling Pregnant Students

Discrimination is particularly severe for one group of students—those who become pregnant. Every year over 200,000 young women under eighteen give birth.[17] Usually these young women are expelled from school at the first sign of pregnancy. Out of 17,000 school districts surveyed in 1970, fewer than one-third offered pregnant school-age girls any education at all.[18] School districts that did allow students to study during pregnancy usually kept them at home or segregated them in special classes for various reasons: on moral grounds, for special protection, or for convenience.[19]

None of these reasons justify denying a young woman the right to regular public education with her peers. There is no evidence that pregnant students are morally contagious. Class attendance poses no greater health hazard to pregnant women than performing a job, doing housework, or caring for other children; all things that women commonly do up until childbirth.

Expulsion compounds the already serious problems of teenage pregnancy. Of every 100 pregnant teenagers who leave school, eighty-five never come back. Rejected, cast out with a child to support and often no salable skills, these teenagers are nine times more likely to commit suicide than their peers.[20]

Eighty-five percent will keep their babies, either to raise an illegitimate child alone or to enter into a early marriage that is three or four times more likely to end in divorce than marriages in any other age groups.[21] Their children are four times more likely to have psychological problems than those with older parents. Among the teenage mothers who remain unmarried, 85 percent go on welfare.[22]

Guidance and Counseling

As a girl prepares to leave secondary school to take a job or to seek further education, school guidance counseling may further dissuade her from striking off in academic or vocational directions which may be her choice but which are usually reserved for men.

Many guidance counselors advise students to do what's "practical." Unfortunately, what is considered practical may lead to a tragic underutilization of women's talents and skills. Counselors may advise girls to go into conventional "women's fields," regardless of their interests or abilities. But, as we have stated above, many girls are interested in other fields.

Sex discrimination in another form of guidance, vocational interest tests, has begun to attract public attention. One test, the Strong Vocational Interest Blank, received widespread attention when cited for sex bias in March, 1972, by the American Personnel and Guidance Association. As the association's resolution calling for the test revision explained:

> The Blanks (SVIB) provide different occupational scores for men and women: women cannot be scored on occupations like certified public accountant, purchasing agent, and public administrator; men cannot be scored on occupations such as medical technologist, recreation leader and physical education teacher.
>
> When the same person takes both tests, the profiles turn out differently: one woman scored high as a dental assistant, physical therapist, and occupational therapist on the woman's profile, and as a physician, psychiatrist and psychologist on the man's form.[23]

BIASES IN POSTSECONDARY EDUCATION

Although more and more women are demanding and gaining access to postsecondary education, the record is not one of consistent progress. The proportion of women undergraduates and professional students grew from 30 percent in 1950 to 41 percent in 1970 but was still smaller than it was in 1930. And women won a higher proportion of the doctorate degrees during the 1920's, 1930's, and 1940's than they did in the 1960's.[24]

According to one study, only half of the female high school graduates qualified for college work actually do go on to college, while 65 percent of the qualified men do.[25] The proportions of women shrink on each step of the educational ladder. Women earn just over half the high school diplomas; but they earn 43 percent of the bachelor's degrees, 40 percent of the master's degrees, and only 13 percent of the doctorates.[26]

Women also have a more difficult time gaining access to top quality education. In the thirty-five undergraduate institutions, both single sex and coeducational, judged the "most selective in the country" by one college handbook, women represented only 29.3 percent of the admissions in 1970. They were only 32 percent of those admitted to the coeducational institutions.[27]

Yet women perform as well or better than their male peers in both the secondary and the undergraduate years. Sex discrimination in admissions, student aid awards and counseling contribute to these disparities.

Admissions

Sex discrimination in admissions—commonplace in public and private institutions, single sex and coeducational—is one obstacle facing women seeking higher education.

Most of the approximately 300 institutions which exclude members of one sex are private, although a few public institutions close their doors to women. Of these, the United States military academies are the most prominent. Because of the single-sex pattern of higher education in Virginia in 1964, the state system that year rejected 21,000 women and not a single male. Since then, the state has changed its policies.[28] Sex discrimination in admissions to public institutions is particularly burdensome, since public education is in general substantially less expensive than private education.

Most students attend coeducational institutions of higher education, and it is in admissions to these schools that discrimination against women is so damaging. Coeducational institutions, both public and private, use various strategies to limit the number of women admitted. Some use quota systems to maintain a steady ratio of male and female students, almost always with women in the minority Cornell University, for example, maintains a male/female ratio of 3:1; Harvard/Radcliffe, 4:1.[29] The main campus at Pennsylvania State University, a public institution, this year ended a long-standing quota of 2.5 men to every woman.[30]

Other institutions simply demand higher admission standards for women than for men. Whatever the system, women usually come out on the short end. As a faculty member at one graduate school commented: "Our general admissions policy has been, if the body is warm and male, take it; if it's female, make sure it's an A-from Bryn Mawr."[31]

Student Aid

Sex discrimination in student aid awards is another roadblock for women seeking higher education. The Educational Testing Service (ETS) recently documented a clear pattern of sex discrimination in student aid. ETS found that women averaged $215 less in student financial aid than men, though women had equal financial need. To compound the problem, men working to defray college costs earned more than female students. This was not only true in off-campus jobs: the biggest disparities were in jobs provided by colleges and universities, where men averaged $300 per year, or 78 percent, more than women.[32]

Women are effectively excluded from certain kinds of scholarship aid. Government scholarships designed to attract men into military service, such as ROTC scholarships, have not been available to women, nor can most women qualify for veterans' benefits. Athletic scholarships, a significant portion of financial aid in some institutions, are limited to men. And many private scholarships and fellowships are designated for men only. Until 1969 New York University Law School, for example, excluded women from competition for Root-Tilden scholarships, generous $10,000 scholarships for "future public leaders," a category which apparently was felt to be suitable only for men.[33]

According to ETS, the only type of student aid where women averaged larger sums than men was in loans—probably because they receive less aid from other sources and must rely on larger loans.[34] Loans are an expensive way of financing an education for anyone, but they represent a particularly heavy burden for women, since women have less earning power than men.

Women who are married or raising children may have particular difficulty securing the aid they need to remain in or return to school. Financial aid officers may feel that these women do not need help, since they have husbands to support them, or that they are probably not serious about obtaining an education. In addition, financial aid is difficult to obtain for part-time study, which poses an additional handicap for women with children who can only attend school part-time.

Counseling

Counseling for women in higher education holds the same hazards it does for younger women in secondary schools. Advisors often urge women to avoid "masculine" academic fields or discourage them from applying to graduate schools where common wisdom has it that it is hard for women to get in. Women are often warned against seeking further education, despite good academic records:

— "Have you ever thought about journalism? (to a student planning to get a Ph.D. in political science). I know a lot of women journalists who do very well."
— "A pretty girl like you will certainly get married. Why don't you stop with an M.A.?"[35]

Biases against women in each of these areas—admissions, student aid and counseling—are typically rationalized by widely-held prejudices and presumptions about women and their needs. It is assumed that some man will always provide for a woman, that women won't complete their education, or that women don't really need an education. As a young widow with a five-year old child who needed a fellowship to continue her studies was told, "You're very attractive. You'll get married again. We have to give fellowships to people who really need them."[36]

In fact, none of these assumptions hold up. Millions of women will remain single, be divorced or widowed, or marry a low wage-earner.[37] According to the data available, women are slightly more likely to complete high school and slightly less likely to complete postsecondary degree programs than men in the same field. The more education a woman has, the more likely she is to hold a job. A study of female Ph.D.'s seven years after receiving their degrees found 91 percent working—81 percent full-time.[38] Moreover, it is shortsighted to suggest that a man needs a college education if he works for pay, while a women doesn't if she works at raising children.

Undoubtedly, many of the myths persist because many people are simply unable to accept women as equals to men. The attitude is perhaps best expressed in a comment of Nathan Pusey while president of Harvard. Upon learning of the end to graduate student deferments during the Vietnam war, Pusey said, "We shall be left with the blind, the lame, and the women."[39]

WOMEN WITH SPECIAL NEEDS ENCOUNTER ADDITIONAL DIFFICULTIES

Because of their special life patterns, many women with family responsibilities experience special difficulties in acquiring an education. For mothers who wish to continue their studies while their children are young, finding adequate, affordable child care is a major problem. Others who interrupt their education to raise children or pay for a husband's education find returning to education limited by such problems as a dearth of part-time study opportunities and by credit transfer problems.

These problems are shared by women at all levels of the socioeconomic scale whether they are looking for basic literacy education, occupational training or retraining, or a high school, undergraduate or graduate degree. Women with families need special services and flexible arrangements few educational institutions have been willing to offer.

Child Care Needs

Students' child care needs have not been adequately met. Day care is not readily available for many people and costs are still prohibitive. While low-cost cooperative day care centers are growing in popularity, adequate child care can be expensive. A recent study of "quality" child care centers estimated average costs at $2,600 per child per year.[40]

A woman with children who is not working must add child care costs to her educational expenses, since she would no longer be at home providing these services free of charge. Without help in shouldering child care costs, large numbers of women must stay home despite a desire to continue their education.

In postsecondary education, demands for child care assistance have exploded within the last three or four years. Child care centers subsidized partially at university expense have begun to appear on campuses. Centers often double as research laboratories for campus scholars and students. However, efforts to date are still grossly insufficient. The American Association of University Women reports that no more than 5 percent of our colleges and universities offer day care services.[41] Some are open only to faculty children; many impose extremely selective admissions criteria to deal with the surplus of applications. Waiting lists are long.[42]

The child care issue has not won much visibility in secondary and vocational schools, perhaps because these schools have traditionally refused responsibility for educating young women with children. With growing recognition that pregnancy and motherhood are not acceptable grounds for denying young people the right to public education, school systems will have to confront the child care issue. Child care services may be essential for keeping young mothers in school.

National statistics on the number of mothers seeking child care assistance in order to attend school are nonexistent. However, we do know that in 1971 over two million college students, 25 percent of the total national enrollment, were married.[43] And over 200,000 women under eighteen have children each year.

Child care services have barely begun to meet the demands, either for women already struggling to balance studies and child care responsibilities or for women who might return to education or training if they had access to acceptable child care.

Part-Time Study Needs

Although not as limiting as lack of access to child care facilities, other hurdles stand in front of the women who wish to return to school, including a dearth of part-time study opportunities. For many women, part-time study is often the only way to combine childrearing with learning. More and more people of both sexes, unable or unwilling to devote full time to education, are demanding access to postsecondary education.

Although no national data are available, part-time study opportunities clearly do not come close to meeting this demand. Part-time vocational or manpower training is extremely rare. Traditional continuing education courses offered part-time usually cannot be credited toward a degree, and many undergraduate schools still close their doors to all part-time students.

Academic Credit Problems

Because families often go where the husbands' opportunities take them, credit transfer problems in higher education are particularly acute among married women. Many institutions refuse to accept transfer credits from other institutions. Even if they accept academic credits already earned, no credit is normally given for the years of experience and learning these women have had outside the classroom.

The Age Handicap

Some institutions discriminate, either openly or covertly, against applicants over a certain age. This policy falls harshly on women hoping to continue their education after raising their children.

Both women and men can benefit from adjustments in conventional institutional practices. The failure of education institutions to respond to the needs of women and men returning to education is an unjust and inexcusable waste of valuable human resources. Not only are these individuals denied fulfillment of their potential, but the institutions themselves suffer by not using the wealth of experience these people have already acquired.

THE EDUCATION SYSTEM AS AN EMPLOYER

Women employed in the education system face discrimination practices just as damaging as those women experience as students. Education, tradition has it, is a woman's field. Women make up the bulk of the nation's teaching staff in the elementary and secondary schools; yet they remain a largely untapped and underutilized source of educational leadership. Women are denied equal pay and equal opportunity for advancement, and they are channeled into a small number of "approved" educational fields. Wherever you look in education, women abound in the lower ranks and there, generally, they stay.

Women returning to careers in education face many of the same obstacles women returning as students encounter. Pregnant teachers, frequently receive the same summary treatment as pregnant students—policies require them to leave the jobs while pregnant, often with no guarantee of a place when they return. Day care services or subsidies are rarely available to employees in education, and part-time employment opportunities are scarce.

Women in Administrative Positions

Elementary and secondary schools are mainly staffed by women, but when teachers are selected to move into the administrative ranks, men are usually chosen. In school year 1970-71, 67 percent of all public school teachers were women, but women constituted:

—31 percent of the department heads,
—15 percent of the principals, and
—0.6 percent of the superintendents.[44]

Presently, only two Chief State School Officers are women—those in Montana and Guam. When women do get into administrative positions, it is usually at the elementary school level where responsibility, pay and status are lower. While 20 percent of the elementary school principals in 1970-71 were female, women were only 3.5 percent of the junior high school principals and 3 percent of the high school principals.[45]

In postsecondary education administration, women are even less visible, but the same pattern holds. Men dominate college and university administration, particularly at the policy-making levels. The National Education Association's 1971-72 survey of higher education institutions found that of 953 presidencies in four-year institutions, women held only thirty-two; the proportion is about the same in two-year colleges.[46] Even some of the women's colleges, which historically guaranteed women opportunities for administrative leadership, have been hiring male presidents in recent years.

Female trustees are rare. A 1970 American Association of University Women survey found that 21 percent of the institutions responding to the survey had not a single female trustee and another 25 percent had only one.[47] The only deanship women were likely to hold was dean of women; only 21 percent of the deans of administration, faculty or instruction were women.[48] Perhaps the most startling statistic was the sex breakdown of head librarians in four-year higher education institutions—in a field 83 percent female, nearly 70 percent of the head librarians were men.

A long tradition of excluding women from top administrative positions in education may discourage some women from aspiring to administrative positions. However, the fact remains that administration is "the way up" in American public education in terms of salary, responsibility and status. It is absurd to conclude that many women year after year voluntarily turn their backs on these hallmarks of advancement.

Discrimination Against Women in Higher Education Facilities

Colleges and universities present an array of obstacles to women who want to teach at that level. Less than one in five faculty members is a woman. A recent study of the University of California at Berkeley pointed out that 23 percent of the university's doctorates in psychology went to women, but the last time a woman had been hired in the psychology department was in 1924.[50] Discrimination in hiring at large and prestigious institutions has forced many women to take jobs in small institutions with lower pay and status and less opportunity for research.

Once women join the faculty, discrimination makes it much harder for them to move up through the ranks than for men. Almost 40 percent of the full-time instructors at four-year institutions are women, but the proportion of women drops with each rise in rank. Women comprise

—21 percent of the assistant professors,
—15 percent of the associate professors, and
— 9 percent of the full professors.[51]

Women are likely to remain on each step of the academic ladder long after their male colleagues with the same qualifications have moved on. While it has been reported that females with doctorates "have somewhat greater academic ability than their male counterparts,"[52] barely half of all women with doctorates and twenty years of academic experience are full professors, 90 percent of the men with the same qualifications have reached that rank.[53]

Taking into account all the possible factors influencing faculty rank, Astin and Bayer concluded in a recent analysis that sex discrimination is an important factor in determining faculty rank—more important than such factors as the number of years employed at the institution, the number of books published, and the number of years since completion of education.[54]

In addition, it appears that the more prestigious and institution the less likely women are to penetrate the upper ranks. At Harvard University, to pick an obvious example, of 411 tenured professors in the Graduate School of Arts and Science in 1970-71, 409 were men.[55]

Salary Discrimination in Education

Institutions of higher education regularly pay women less than men of equal rank. In terms of median salaries by rank, women instructors earn $510 per year less than male instructors, and women full-time professors earn $1,762 per year less than their male counterparts.[56] And as time goes on, the gap is widening.

Astin and Bayer found that sex was a better independent

predictor of salary than such factors as years of professional employment and type of advanced degree. The authors reported that by 1968-69 standards, female faculty members should receive an average of $1,000 a year more just to equalize their salaries with those of their male colleagues of equal rank and experience.[57] This is an extremely conservative estimate, since it does not take into account financial inequities attributable to other kinds of discrimination: in promotions, opportunities for research, hiring by high-paying institutions, and other factors.

At present no data are collected on teacher salaries in elementary and secondary schools. However, in some states, elementary and secondary schools are prohibited by statute from paying women less than men of equal rank. In vocational education the median salary in 1969 for female teachers for all levels combined was $1,158 less than for men; women earned only 87 percent as much as their male counterparts.[58]

Sex Typing By Field

Within the education professions, positions are highly sex-typed. Women tend to be clustered in certain fields; men in others. Women overwhelmingly dominate early childhood education, elementary education, and special education. They are 92 percent of the school librarians. In vocational education, most of the teachers in the health occupations, home economics, and office occupations are women. At the lowest end of the professional scale, almost all teacher aides and other educational paraprofessionals are female.

Men, on the other hand, have always dominated teaching positions in mathematics, the sciences, law, medicine and engineering. In vocational education teaching in agriculture, distributive education, technical education and trades and industry has been predominantly male.

In recent years, educators have begun to wage an energetic campaign to attract men into the fields of education customarily dominated by women. In some of these fields, the proportion of men has increased, stimulated perhaps by tight job markets elsewhere. If the same energy were devoted to bringing women into male-dominated fields, a few years could bring substantial changes.

Nonprofessionals in Education

Women employed as nonprofessionals experience similar discrimination in hiring, advancement and pay. HEW's Office for Civil Rights has turned up numerous cases of sex discrimination against nonprofessional employees. In one institution, custodial employees were divided by sex into "maids" and "janitors." Each had the same duties, but maids were paid substantially less. In another, four pay levels were created for the job of clerk; white males received the highest pay, black males next highest, white females came after that, and black females were last. All of them had to have the same qualifications and perform the same work.

Career ladders for nonprofessionals and paraprofessionals are practically nonexistent. Despite growing popularity of teacher aides, few school systems offer these people, almost always women, the chance for training and advancement to professional responsibility and status. Like most employers, few education institutions have begun to face up to the need for career ladders to enable nonprofessional office workers to move into the professional office jobs.

RESEARCH AND DEVELOPMENT: HELP OR HINDRANCE?

Research and development can offer valuable insights and useful tools for tackling our most perplexing problems. Despite their potential, research and development to date have contributed little to our ability to solve one of education's most serious inequities: systematic discrimination against the female sex. In general, research and development people have shown only slight interest in exploring sex biases or testing ways of overcoming them. Moreover, studies too often reflect the anti-female biases of researchers.

Exploring Sexism through Research and Development

It is encouraging to note that there are increasing signs of interest in research relating to sex biases, particularly among female scholars. However, remarkably little scholarly work has been done on sex discrimination itself—either on the precise nature and extent of sex bias within the education system, its roots, or its effects. An ERIC search for research materials on sex discrimination produced only twelve items, none containing any empirical results.[59] Too much of our information on sex discrimination is piecemeal, anecdotal, or out of date.

Researchers have produced some information on sex differences and sex role development. They often report findings on differences and similarities between males and females in play behavior, learning styles, interactions with teachers and in other situations. Where differences exist, causes are rarely explored. We still lack empirical evidence on the extent to which these differences are biologically or culturally determined.

Research on the way children develop concepts of appropriate sex role behavior has had similar limitations. There is (as we noted earlier) evidence that as children go through school, they progressively acquire clearer and more rigid ideas about what is expected of males and females. But we do not know to what extent schooling may be responsible or which aspects of the educational experience have the strongest influence on children's concepts of appropriate sex roles.

Much of the research on sex role stereotypes has another weakness: many studies reflect the researcher's assumption that accepting traditional masculine/feminine role differences is essential to a child's healthy development. In fact, learning all the "cannots" and "must nots" traditionally associated with being female in this society can be a crippling experience. Although there have been a few extremely provocative studies on this problem, many of the studies of sex role development appear to be motivated by a desire to see that boys and girls develop "proper" sex role concepts. For instance, researchers studying the effects of female teachers on boys frequently express a concern that boys may fail to develop "appropriate" sex role identification without male teachers as models.[60]

Unless the necessary research is put to use, it will provide little help to children in classrooms. It must be accompanied by the products of development: for instance, new curricula, teaching approaches, whole new forms and models that can be put to use in real educational settings. As matters stand, curriculum materials and teacher training techniques aimed at helping teachers avoid sexist behavior are virtually nonexistent. A few recent education experiments do have particular significance for women, e.g. a home-community based career education model and nonresident college degree programs with credit for nonacademic experience. However, serious attempts to tackle some of the most basic problems, such as techniques to counter sex role stereotyping in the early preschool and school years, are lacking.

Biased Questionnaires

In addition to the dearth of helpful research and development relating to sex stereotypes and biases, many studies contain sex biases which distort findings and produce knowledge of little or no use in solving problems of discriminating against women. Even worse, these studies may reinforce popular misconceptions about women and encourage educational decisions harmful to them. Sometimes, for example, biases are based on the outdated assumption that woman's proper role is homemaker and dependent. Others seem to reflect attitudes that women, their lives and aspirations—and barriers to those aspirations—are not important enough to be studied.

Sex biases can be found in the kinds of questions researchers ask the population being studied. *Project TALENT*, a major twenty-year longitudinal study of high school students which began with Office of Education support in 1960, offers some examples. The original questionnaire sent out to students recognized that mothers may work and that they may be chief family wage earners. But the questions about responsibilities on the job were limited to fathers' jobs. The questionnaire also included questions relating "your (or your future husband's) " salary to amounts of life insurance, savings and investments. Male students could not include a wife's expected income; female students could not consider combined incomes of self and spouse.[61]

Another example turned up recently in a draft questionnaire prepared for another major longitudinal study now in progress with NCES support.[62] A special questionnaire for those neither in school nor employed reflected a number of highly unscientific assumptions about the role of women. The researchers assumed that everyone who was not employed and not in school was a full-time homemaker and female. The questionnaire repeatedly referred to "your husband," although there are men who by choice or necessity stay home, tending house and/or children. Respondents were also asked what vocational training they would prefer, and the choices were all occupations traditionally attracting large numbers of women: secretarial, dental assistant, food services, beautician, child care. Another question asked whether respondents had taken noncredit adult education courses—courses for credit were not included, implying that women in the home would not be interested in academic education for credit. Fortunately, NCES recognized the problems with this questionnaire, and it has never been used. It is a useful example, however, of the kind of biases that creep into ostensibly "objective" and "scientific" research.

Single Sex Studies

Researchers sometimes pick members of one sex or the other as subjects for study. On the basis of an extensive ERIC search, the task force found that this practice tends to produce distorted information in areas of great importance to women. In the abstracts surveyed, single sex studies were more than two times as likely to use males as females. Seventy-eight dealt with males only and thirty-four dealt only with females. Again, most of the thirty-four abstracts on women did not contain empirical studies, while most of the ones on males did report study results.

Researchers are also much more likely to use males rather than females as a basis for generalizing about the whole population. In our review of the ERIC files, for example, less than half the titles of male-only studies indicated that only men had been studied, while more than three fourths of the titles of female-only entries filed indicated that only females had been studied.

The tendency of researchers to draw general conclusions from a study of males is particularly disturbing and particularly prevalent in research in areas of special importance to women, or where important differences can be expected between men and women. In the abstracts reviewed, male-only studies focused most often on careers, the poor, and the emotionally and physically handicapped. Slow readers, school dropouts, underachievers, the physically fit, and delinquents were also the topics of male-only studies.

Few of the female-only abstracts dealt with careers. None of the other topics appeared in female-only studies except delinquency, which rated a study on "clothing fabric selection" among delinquent girls. There were no studies of female dropouts, no studies of poor or ethnic minority females, and no studies of handicapped or underachieving females.

Single sex studies may also reflect faulty assumptions that males have a corner on the problem or issue under study: "Women don't usually work," or "It's really black males who have the problems," or "Most dropouts are male." None of these assumptions are true. Women do usually work, black women are subject to both sex and racial discrimination and have extremely serious problems, boys are only slightly more likely to drop out. It is time researchers understood that women too have pressing needs and began affording them the same attention as men.

The tendency of educational researchers to focus on males makes designing education programs that meet women's needs much harder. A great deal of research has been undertaken on the theory that the knowledge gained can eventually be put to use in changing educational practice. Biased research put to use cannot help but lead to biased educational approaches.

From even a brief look at the status of women in education, it is abundantly clear that education contributes its share to the exploitation of women. Through its system of formal education, society should seek both to nurture young minds and to open doors to lifelong opportunities. On both counts, education is failing the female sex.

CHAPTER 11

CAREER ROLES IN GUIDANCE COUNSELING

DOROTHY B. FLOYD

Introduction
What Is Counseling?
Conditions and Problems Contributing to an Increasing Need
    for Counseling and Personnel
Consideration of Qualifications and Preparation
Roles and Functions of the School Counselor
Training Opportunities in Counseling
Job Opportunities in Counseling
Problems Young Female Adolescents Face in Considering
    Counseling as a Career
Outlook in Counseling
Summary
References

INTRODUCTION

Wanted: A school guidance counselor

Desired Qualities

Sex: Female

Personal Assets: Must be alert and knowledgeable, must possess a healthy self-concept; must be patient, consistent, flexible, honest and open-minded; must be physically and mentally sound; must exemplify strength, wisdom, good judgment, trust, empathy and confidence; must believe in and have respect for the individual worth

170

Career Roles in Guidance Counseling

of all human beings; must be able to interact with individuals and groups of individuals; must like working with people.

Formal Education: Baccalaureate Degree; Master's Degree in Education; Master's Degree in Guidance and Counseling.

Further Training: (Workshops, In-service, Institutes, Seminars, etc):

Modern Trends in Occupations; Curriculum Alterations; Behavioral and Sensitivity Training; Group Techniques; Leadership Training; Interviewing Techniques; Behavior Modification Training; Problems of the Culturally Disadvantaged; Drugs; I.B.M.; and Audio-Visual Aids.

Work Experience: Three or more years as a successful classroom teacher; two or more years of work experience in other occupations (cashier, waitress, sales clerk, sewing machine operator, file clerk, assembly line worker) ; some experience as director and/or advisor of group activities; student council; honor society; chorus; dance groups; cheerleaders; red cross; 4-H; scouts; class advisor, etc.

THE ABOVE STATEMENT describing the desired qualities of a school counselor is not an effort to discourage entrance into the counseling profession. It is an exaggerated attempt to emphasize the seriousness with which one should approach the selection of a vocation. The description used is representative of the actual innate and developed qualities plus the accumulated experiences of the writer who feels that the selection of a career is one of the supreme moments in one's life because her future is charted through the choice she makes.

The objective of this chapter is to set forth a realistic format for young female adolescents to review during the process of career selection. Consideration will be given to the following areas: a general statement concerning the definition of guidance counseling; conditions and problems contributing to the growing need for counselors; the importance of the qualifications of the person who is considering counseling as a career; the roles and functions of the counselor; training opportunities; job opportunities; problems young females face in the area of guidance and counseling; and future outlook in the field. Hopefully, this effort will help to provide some insight for the adolescent female who is considering counseling as a vocation.

WHAT IS COUNSELING?

If a survey were conducted in a given community in quest of a definition for counseling, the findings would probably reveal a wide range of expressions. An elementary school pupil may perceive counseling as a game where he gets to call the shots. To a junior high schooler, it may be viewed as an authentic excuse to get out of class. A senior high school pupil may refer to such as encounter a "present help in the time of trouble." The college student may consider this as a venture that provides an apportunity to flirt with the counselor or just a "happening." A parent's view may range between a necessity and a waste of time. The alcoholic and the drug addict may see such an encounter as an avenue leading to hopelessness or salvation. The variability of these expressions is indicative of the different ways people perceive counseling. So, then, what is counseling?

There are many theoretical definitions and descriptions for the term cited by various authorities for people who are already in the process of becoming counselors. However, for the adolescent who is considering counseling as a career, a more picturesque definition is necessary. It should describe the counseling role as an entity in terms of its many aspects. With this in mind, the writer has coined the following definition.

> Counseling is a process which requires the art of using a stack of personal assets, a storehouse of knowledge, and a series of techniques in a wide variety of combinations in order to provide effective helping relations and services in a given setting, for individuals who need, want and seek help in solving their problems.

As the chapter progresses, this definition should take on more latitude and become more meaningful to the reader.

CONDITIONS AND PROBLEMS CONTRIBUTING TO AN INCREASING NEED FOR COUNSELING PERSONNEL

In recent years, the impact of rapid change generated by America's social revolution has given rise to numerous conditions and problems that are indicative of an increasing need for counseling services in the school and in the community. The pressure of freedom-seeking groups, especially among older adolescents and young adults, has permeated our entire society—the beatniks, flower children, and hippies seeking a new way of life; the Civil Rights movement with blacks seeking freedom from oppression and segregation in terms of education, housing and employment; women seeking liberation from the prejudices of men; war-haters seeking freedom from enlistment in the armed services; and individuals, in general, seeking freedom in life styles, sex indulgence and drug use.

Among older adult groups the acceptance of, the adjustment to, and the methods of facilitating some of these changes have encountered "die hard" opposition, thereby arousing unhealthy feelings. This adds another dimension to an already complicated situation.

The most difficult group to cope with is that of the very young adolescents whose lack of judgment cause them to misinterpret this supposedly new freedom. As a result, we are now experiencing what may be called the Teenage Era of the Sixteen Syndrome. Sixteen years of age has been dubbed the magic chronological number. It is the age when one becomes eligible for driver license, worker's permit, dating, and it marks the end of compulsory school attendance.

Change, in its broadest sense, has affected every facet of adolescent life. Manners are fast becoming passé. Adult supervision is scoffed upon. Adult vices are accepted by many as a way of life. Self-direction has been overpowered by the wishes of the group. Free sex and the use of drugs are fast becoming the rule rather than the exception. Petty crime has almost become a status symbol.

With these and other problems, developmental in nature, facing today's youth, could there be any doubt that there is a tremendous need for help?

CONSIDERATION OF QUALIFICATIONS AND PREPARATION

An awareness of our social problems and their effect upon the world of work is imperative if an individual is to make a realistic career choice. This kind of knowledge provides a basis for objective self-analysis, a serious review of the educational requirements, and a good look at the kinds of experiences which might be an asset to the person making the decision.

The Appraisal of Personal Assets

Generally, the kinds of work may be divided into three groups: working with ideas, working with things, and working with people. Specifically, all work involves all three areas to some degree with at least one category highly emphasized. Counseling is unique in that it requires a great deal of work with both ideas and things although it is basically a "people" kind of work. Therefore, a wide range of positive personal assets is required.

The student who is considering guidance and counseling as a vocation may very well begin by asking herself some important personal questions such as

Who am I?
How do I see myself as an individual?
What are my mental capabilities?
Am I alert?
Am I in good condition physically and mentally?
What are my assets and limitations?
Am I trustworthy?
Do I display a high level of good judgment?
Do I exemplify strength, courage, wisdom, patience and empathy?
How flexible am I?
Am I able to use my strengths to an advantage?
Can I accept my weaknesses?
What are my likes and dislikes?
Do I really like people?
Am I capable of understanding and accepting people as they are?
Do I believe in and have respect for the individual worth of all human beings?
Do I like working with people?

The answers to these and similar questions must be sought in order to provide an awareness of self which is another imperative venture in choosing a career.

Preparation and Certification

Today, our present social crisis demands the best preparation possible for students who plan to enter the counseling profession.

With the advent of new problematic dimensions in our society such as drug use, free sex, and technology, it has become necessary to revise and broaden counselor education programs. An effort in this direction is being made in various parts of the country through pilot programs which have been designed to test new approaches to counselor training. However, the basic requirements have not changed.

Educational Preparation

Generally, a wide range of interests and a broad educational background are expected if the counselor is to work effectively with students who need help in various problem areas. Such a background should include a broad knowledge including English grammar and composition, biological sciences, the languages, general psychology, mathematics, philosophy, economics, sociology, history, art and music. Knowledge of this sort should be accumulated during high school and undergraduate college years.

Specific counselor training background should include such areas as Theories of Guidance and Counseling, Techniques in Counseling, Personality Development, Human Development, Childhood and Adolescent Psychology, Psychology of Abnormal Behavior, Psychometric Instruments, Educational Statistics, Behavorial Science, Social Psychology, Administration of Psychological Tests, Educational Research, Counseling Ethics, Counseling Law, Problems of the Disadvantaged, Occupational Information, Psychology of Careers, and Supervised Practicum.

Certification

Since each state sets up its own certification laws, requirements vary considerably from one state to another. However, some basic requirements are consistent in all states. All states require a baccalaureate degree plus a master's degree or an equivalent in Counselor Education. The states vary somewhat in their requirements of teaching experience and work experience.

Some factors contributing to this variation in certification requirements may be the demand for counselors, the use of classroom teachers as part-time counselors, the lack of funds for the employment of certified counselors, and the introduction of the fifth year counselor program. In the five-year program the student bypasses classroom teaching experience and goes directly into counseling.

Although many authorities may not agree, the writer finds it highly inconceivable that one would consider going into school counseling without some background in classroom teaching. Not only can such an experience, if successful, provide a foundation for better insight into the problems of our youth and how to deal with them, but it can also create a sympathetic undertsanding for the problems classroom teachers face. Knowledge and understandings of this sort enhance the level of competency in counseling.

A multitude of advantages may be derived from classroom teaching. They include the opportunity to

1. Learn to accept students as individuals.
2. Become aware of individual differences.
3. Recognize individual differences (mental ability; economic, cultural, social background).
4. Learn the importance of home visitation.
5. Learn how to communicate with parents.
6. Learn the importance of communicating with parents.
7. Experiment with individual and group procedures in teaching.
8. Observe different styles of learning.
9. Observe individual strengths and weaknesses.
10. Discover and develop leadership qualities.
11. Discover sepecial abilities.
12. Observe childhood and/or adolescent behavior.
13. Develop skills.
14. Discover potentials.
15. Learn to create conducive climates.
16. Utilize student resources.
17. Experiment with various techniques and methods in teaching content materials.
18. Learn to share ideas and materials with other teachers.
19. Learn how to build rapport with students and teachers.
20. Learn the school network and how it operates.

Other kinds of work experience can provide a great deal of first-hand knowledge that can be most valuable to the counselor in disseminating occupational information, working with students who are seeking jobs, and working with teachers. Some advantages of this experience are

1. A broader knowledge of the applying procedure.
2. First-hand knowledge of testing procedures and the kinds of test used.
3. First-hand information regarding the job description, required skills, the importance of the employer-employee relationship, job hazards, opportunity for advancement, wages, etc.

Counselor preparation does not end with certification. If so, the counselor will eventually become static, and there is no place for a static counselor in a changing society. Many provisions are made for counselors to keep abreast with changes through in-service training, workshops, seminars, etc. Credits earned may be used to update certificates, which is a periodic requirement. Professional organizations also keep counselors abreast through their periodic publications. These organizations operate at the national, state and local levels.

Organizational Affiliations

The professional organization for counselors is the American Personnel and Guidance Association (APGA). It is a uniting force for eight divisions. Association for Counselor Education and Supervision (ACES), American School Counselor Association, (ASCA), National Vocational Guidance Association (NVGA), are the divisions counselors can benefit from directly. Their publications provide current developments in the field so members can keep abreast with current issues. Every counselor should seek membership to promote constant effectiveness. The journals published are *Personnel and Guidance Journal* (APGA), *Journal of College Student Personnel* (ACES), *The School Counselor* (ASCA), and *Vocational Guidance Quarterly* (NVGA).

ROLES AND FUNCTIONS OF THE SCHOOL COUNSELOR

There are four levels of counseling within the school setting: elementary, junior high school or middle school, senior high school, and college. Each level is representative of a specific stage in human development that has problematic characteristics of its own. The areas of concentration in a given school must be determined, to a great extent, by the level at which the counselor is employed, the socio-economic background of the student population, and the attitudes of the school staff and the community.

In any school, the roles and functions of the counselor constitute an intricate network that is woven into the fabric of the overall school program. This makes the counselor unique in terms of latitude and opportunity. Latitude refers to the area in which the counselor is free to move and the people with whom she is free to work—the administrators, the teachers, the students, the parents, and other supporting agencies. Opportunity refers to the kinds of resources brought in by the counselor and their use in helping, in every way possible, to bring about positive change.

In order to reach a high level of competency in counseling, there are several abilities the counselor must have at her disposal. John W. Loughary (1971) has them outlined in his article "To Grow or Not to Grow":

1. The ability to read and understand manuals, bulletins, schedules, reports, and other documents. Also familiarity with a variety of styles of organizing and presenting such materials.
2. The ability to generate understandable written communication for a variety of audiences and purposes.
3. A basic knowledge of available audio-visual media, skills involved in their use, and their potential impact and uses regarding changing behavior.
4. The ability to read, interpret and draw conclusions from statistical data presented in charts or diagram forms and the ability to develop statistical presentations from raw data.
5. The ability to use various interviewing techniques to obtain information.
6. The ability to develop rational plans for accomplishing specific objectives.
7. The ability to devise and use behavior which reinforces the desired behavior in others.
8. The ability to define objectives.
9. The ability to summarize and draw conclusions from nonstatistical data.

10. A knowledge of several methods of organizational structure and what each is intended to achieve.

The emphasis placed on the above qualities is an effort to reinforce the need for self-appraisal and to clarify the need for such abilities in terms of the different roles the school counselor must assume.

Guidance and counseling has reached an all-time high in its growth and popularity and is still growing. There is evidence of future specializing where a counselor may prepare for a special phase in school counseling. There is also evidence that the profession may become more closely allied with psychology. But, at the present, counselors are expected to assume several types of responsibilities.

Students who have the idea that all the counselor does is sit at a desk in the comfort of her office, wave a magic wand, and all's well are in for a shock. This stereotype role of the counselor is fast becoming a myth. Students who think the counselor does nothing but counsel are also victims of a false impression.

To explain in detail everything a counselor does is next to an impossibility, but here is a general descriptions of the kinds of roles one must assume within the realm of school counseilng:

1. *Planner—* of the guidance program and curriculum in relation to student needs.
2. *Organizer—* of programs, groups activities, schedules, etc.
3. *Consultant—* to the administrative staff, teachers, parents, and other school-related agencies.
4. *Coordinator—* of the accumulation of useful student information, placement, community school-related services, testing programs, etc.
5. *Collector and Dissiminator—* of all kinds of information (educational, vocational, etc.).
6. *Placement Officer—* adjusts schedules, helps students make appropriate choices, helps students in making transitions from one school level to another.

7. *Referral Officer—* makes referrals to the school nurse, attendance officers, psychological services, mental health and social workers, and other agencies.

8. *Facilitator—* makes progress through negotiation and advocation, etc. Aids in making things work.

9. *Researcher—* collects, analyzes, organizes and presents data test results, follow-ups, and other evaluative materials.

10. *Counselor—* conducts the one-to-one relationship between the counselor and counselee(s) with concentration in helping the counselee to identify his feelings, deal with his feelings in terms of his environment, make self-appraisal of experiences, explore possibilities, make decisions, make plans and evaluate progress, etc.

Counseling was purposely placed last in the above sequence because it is the foundation upon which all of the other roles rest. A counseling situation may grow out of any of the counselor's involvements. The episode below is indicative of one of the writer's experiences.

This experience involves two ninth grade boys. Both were fourteen years old, more physically mature and academically talented than the average fourteen-year-old youngster. These boys were good friends and each of them had an IQ far above average. They were placed in Special Abilities and Talents (SAT) classes and had done some very outstanding work. Both boys had poor attendance records since seventh grade which grew progressively worse. Referrals were made to the attendance officer and the social worker, conferences were held with their parents who were ready to give up, and some of their teachers came in for consultation seeking help regarding their attendance.

The real problem was revealed through counseling. It was discovered that these boys had a hangup about taking physical education which is required all three years in junior high school. One of them refused to dress out and participate because he was not as agile as most of the boys in his class, so he was teased a great deal. The other had a hangup regarding the physical education program and felt that the course was not designed to meet his needs.

Consultation with the principal was the writer's next move. She explained the existing circumstances surrounding the problems and negotiated, in their behalf, for latitude in alternatives. Conferences were arranged so the boys could present their cases to the principal who consented to let them change their schedules on a temporary basis because both students threatened to drop out of school as soon as they became sixteen if they were forced to remain in P. E. classes. One student chose to assist the librarian and the other chose to assist a teacher in creative writing.

During and after a trial period their attendance became perfect. The teachers to whom they were assigned were highly pleased with their performance. Their academic performance improved, and they were more satisfied with school life. Near the end of the school year these students consented to participate in a video taping session on "The Prospective School Dropout" which was shown on several occasions over educational television.

Both boys graduated from senior high school this year (1973) with excellent records in advanced and regular courses. The one who assisted in creative writing has written several articles that were published in the school paper and the local newspaper. He received honorable mention on his test performance and he plans to attend one of the local universities this fall. The other student was quite optimistic about a scholarship offered by the firm where his father is employed. He also plans to enroll in college in the fall.

The above episode is characteristic of the counselor's involvement. It involved the students, teachers, parents, attendance officers, social workers, principal, educational T.V. staff members, set workers at the T.V. station, counselors at the senior high school. The process involved consultation, referral, gathering data, recommendations, placement, coordination, cooperation, and follow-up.

This is just one of the many examples of the work of the counselor that proved to be successful. However, there are many more that are not as successful, yet some progress is made. There are still other attempts that fail miserably from the outset. These are usually referred to another counselor or to another person who might be able to help the student.

TRAINING OPPORTUNITIES IN COUNSELING

Undergraduate Training Opportunities

Formal training for counselors, like any other profession, begins with undergraduate college preparation. This means that a student must complete a four-year college program with a specific major. Home economics majors, for example, may enter into counseling with relative ease due to the wide range of subject matter required: family living, nutrition, chemistry, bacteriology, zoology, physics, anatomy, child care, health, housing, finance and budgeting, foods, clothing, art, design, etc. The student's major may be greatly enhanced by the acquisition of a minor or a second major such as math or social studies and interests such as music, drama, student publications or student government.

Training at this level may be obtained from any of the accredited colleges and universities throughout the United States. These institutions range from community colleges with a two-year college program to colleges and universities with the fifth and sixth year programs.

Counselor Training Opportunities

Many students go directly into the world of work upon completion of the four years of college preparation. For those who wish to go into counseling after working a while, several institutions of higher learning have set up programs to meet their needs. These programs are designed to provide specialized counselor training beyond the bachelor's degree which will lead to counselor certification. Other programs are designed for students who wish to achieve the doctorate level in counseling.

In-Service Training Opportunities

Additional opportunities in counselor training are provided through in-service programs in the form of workshops, institutes, seminars, etc. These programs provide continuous growth for counselors who are currently employed and are funded at the national, state and local levels. Many of these in-service programs are tuition-free and pay stipends to the participants. Others are available at moderate costs.

Counselors may also keep abreast with current changes and new methods through the publications of the various professional associations. All counselors are encouraged to maintain membership in at least one division along with American Personnel and Guidance Association membership.

Information regarding colleges and universities, entrance requirements, course offerings, cost, etc., should be available in every senior high school guidance center.

JOB OPPORTUNITIES IN COUNSELING

Although school counseling has been emphasized throughout this chapter, it is by no means the only opportunity in counseling or counseling related vocations. Listed below are some alternative opportunities.

Public Schools

Counselor — Elementary level
Secondary level (Junior High School
and Senior High School)

These counselors assist individual students and groups of students through counseling; appraising aptitudes, abilities, interests, and personality characteristics. They also assist students in making wise educational and vocational plans. Other activities include collecting, organizing and analyzing information about individual students through records, tests, interviews, questionnaires, autobiographies. In addition, they collect, organize and disseminate occupational information. Other titles used for the school counselor are vocational counselor, head counselor, student counselor, social director, dean of girls, etc.

College Level

Dean of Women
Director of Placement
Placement Officer
Director of Student Affairs
Social Director
Residence Counselor
Foreign Student Advisor

Clinical
Psychologist
Psychological Counselor
Personal Advisor
Personal Adjustment Counselor, etc.

Remedial Specialists
Reading
Speech Correction
Education for Slow Learners
Education for the Physically Handicapped
Therapeutic Specialists

Other Opportunities in Counseling
Vocational-Rehabilitation
Employment
Business
Industry
Corrective Institutions
Mental Institutions
Juvenile Centers
YWCA
Recreation and Camps
Church
Armed Forces
Drug Centers
Family Service

In many instances, the school counselor works very closely with these community agencies in assisting students with their problems.

PROBLEMS YOUNG FEMALE ADOLESCENTS FACE IN CONSIDERING COUNSELING AS A CAREER

Choosing a career is a very complex process which covers a wide time block in the life of the student making the choice. This process requires a great deal of insight on the part of the individual in terms of personal and educational problems, as well as vocational problems. In addition to these, there are others—problems of adolescence and those growing out of societal and technological changes. What effect do these problems have upon adolescent females who are beginning to think about counseling as a career? What are some of the problems they may expect to face?

Problems in Personal Assessment

In making a realistic career choice, an accurate self-appraisal is necessary. An analysis of personal characteristics should be made in relation to the vocation under consideration. This may be a difficult task for the young female adolescent who is still maturing, altering her self-concept and changing her outlook on life in general. By the time she completes high school, she may see herself completely different than she did in junior high school. The danger of assessing personal qualities based on premature criteria may cause a young girl to make an unwise career selection. To prevent this problem, it is highly essential that the continuous evaluation of personal assets become a permanent part of the overall selection process.

There are other problems which are quite prevalent among girls who are experiencing early and middle adolescence. For example, a girl may possess many positive personality characteristics and an above average IQ, but her friends may have far less to offer in these areas. In order to retain the friendship and acceptance of her peer group, she may be willing to deny the existence of her potentials until it is almost too late to recover from the poor record she has acquired. Another example is the girl whose personal assets are not as positive as those of her friends, but she struggles to maintain her status with the group. She refuses to accept her weaknesses as individual differences; consequently, her attitude may become negatively warped or she may begin to suffer from emotional problems when she finds herself falling farther and farther behind.

Problems in Educational Planning

Since effective counseling is highly dependent on a strong and varied educational background, educational planning is essential even at the high school level. Courses must be carefully planned and successfully completed in order to meet the necessary requirements for college entrance. There are many built-in problems at the high school level that can interfere with the educational objectives of a young girl to steer her temporarily or permanently off course.

1. The availability of part-time work through vocational programs in the school provide the opportunity for immediate income for a new wardrobe or for payments on an automobile.
2. The opportunity to take a limited number of courses provides an excuse to leave school early in order to go to a friend's "pad" for an afternoon party.
3. The option of choosing "sop" courses that have little value instead of the solid academics needed for college.
4. The freedom to cut classes in order to "hang out" in the student lounge with friends at the expense of a failing grade which dulls chances for college acceptance.
5. The existence of poor student-teacher relationships where the student ends up being the loser in a number of ways.
6. The lack of student-counselor relationship which leaves the student uninformed in terms of the necessary high school course selections; the necessary test requirements; methods of selecting a college to meet the students needs; applying procedures and deadlines; available scholarships and other financial aids, etc.

Although these problems apply to students in general, they are compounded for black students who are more likely to cop out due to the pressures and prejudices of desegregation. First of all, they must cope with a system that does not necessarily want to help them. Then, there are many white teachers who expect them to achieve at a lower level than white children. Many white students, teachers and parents look upon them with the preconceived notion that all blacks are inferior. Too frequently, the white counselors find it impossible to relate to them in any role other than that of the troublemaker. These and similar problems grossly account for the negative attitudes and failures of many black students with average and above average intelligence.

Problems Relating to Sex

The role of women in the world of work has been constantly changing since World War II. In recent years, greater progress has been made in that direction through the pressures of the Women's Liberation Movement. As a result women are becoming a more important part of America's labor force. They are employed in many occupations once assigned to men: engineering, automotive mechanics, airplane pilots, construction workers, etc. Counseling, especially school counseling, does not suffer from prejudices against women in general since there seems to be more women than men in the profession. One of the greatest conflicts may very well be a struggle between marriage and a career.

Although attitudes toward the employment of women have changed, a few old myths and ideologies still exist in our society and in the minds of girls and women. These attitudes imply that

1. A woman's place is in the home and she should be contented with her homemaking, child-bearing and child-rearing role.
2. Women are too frivolous for academic endeavors. Sooner or later, they will get married and settle down.
3. Men do not approve of intelligent women. They feel that marriage and a career cannot be managed effectively.
4. There are certain jobs designed specifically for women and others are designed strictly for men.

Female counselors who are married and are successful in their work have proved that the marriage-career can be solved. Their success has helped to dismantle the old myths regarding women and their role in society. Therefore, they are in a position to facilitate more realistic choices in relation to the female client's academic potentials and achievement.

Problems Within The Counseling Profession

Every career has its problems resulting from circumstances and relationships within the confines of the occupational setting, and counseling is no exception. These problems may be directly related to an individual's personality, race, sex, relationships with others, etc. The success with which one can deal with such problems is dependent upon a number of factors: an awareness of the problems; self-confidence in dealing with the problems; and the initiative to introduce alternative solutions to the problems, etc.

Some of the problem areas in counseling are listed below.

Educational Opportunities

Although there is a wide range of available educational opportunities in counseling, many factors can enter to limit their assessibility to the female who would like to take advantage of them.

1. The counselor's marital status, the number of children in her family, and her husband's attitude toward her career.
2. The location of the institution and the time the opportunity is available in relation to the work schedule of the counselor. Some systems do not provide leaves during regular terms.
3. Counselors moving up from the classroom must either take a year off from work to acquire necessary credits for certification or attend evening and summer classes.
4. The enrollment limitations and the screening of enrollees prevent many counselors from taking advantage of available opportunities.
5. The quota system, which is characteristic of the desegregation effort, denies many black counselors an equal opportunity to participate in some instances.

Job Opportunities

Generally, counseling is a growing profession and the need for counselors is steadily increasing. However, there are some problems in this area which might affect the female counselor. A few of these problems are listed below.

1. The limited number of counselors allotted to a given system or to an individual school or institution.
2. Specific requests for male counselors.
3. The number of available qualified applicants.
4. The transient tendencies of the applicant.
5. The desegregation quota used in hiring black counselors.

Relationships

Within the school or within any institution, the success of the counselor is dependent, to a great extent, upon the kind of relationship she establishes with her clients, employer, co-workers, etc. This can easily become one of the greatest problem areas, especially for black counselors. The bases for these problems might very well be the conflicting roles of the counselor as seen by the administrator, the teaching staff, the parents, the student, the community, and the counselor. Here, again, desegregation has compounded the problems of the black counselor the same as it has for black students.

1. The lack of cooperation, on the part of some teachers, in understanding and accepting their role in helping students.
2. The refusal, on the part of some staff members, to accept help offered by the counselor to alleviate classroom problems and to develop better techniques for meeting the needs of the students.
3. The lack of confidentiality on the part of some teachers regarding students and other staff members.
4. The use of negative data, by some staff members, to initiate and support negative attitudes toward some students.
5. The referral of black students to black counselors for disciplinary problems.
6. Some staff members teaming up against a single student to make sure he fails or setting up provocated incidents to make sure he gets suspended.
7. The inability of many white counselors to relate to black students due to preconceived ideas about all blacks.
8. The preconceived notion that all black counselors and all black students come from poverty-stricken families with

disadvantaged backgrounds which automatically makes them inferior to all whites.

9. The inability of some principals and teachers to understand and accept the different levels of maturity the students experience.
10. The consistency with which the counselor must re-evaluate her self-concept and other personal assets in order to cope with the pressure these problems create.

OUTLOOK IN COUNSELING

Counseling is a growing profession that has penetrated practically every phase of our society. Even though it has not been fully developed in some areas, trends point in that direction. The problems in our society and new developments in the field imply

1. An increasing need for well-prepared school counselors and college student personnel.
2. The emergence of the counselor specialist.
3. Wider use of technology in counseling.
4. More consideration given to counseling with the elderly.
5. A greater need for premarriage counseling.
6. An increasing need for counseling in the areas of drug addiction and alcoholism.

SUMMARY

Choosing a career is a complex, time-consuming process. It requires a great deal of insight on the part of the individual who is making the choice. The young adolescent female who is considering counseling as a vocation should be aware of societal and technological changes, the problems of adolescence, her personal assets, educational opportunities in counseling, job opportunities in counseling, some of the problems counselors face, and some idea as to where the career is headed.

The girl who selects counseling as a career must possess a clear knowledge of who she is—that is, what makes her tick; where she is going—the maturity and insight necessary to understand the time required for preparation and the direction her selected course will lead; and how she will get there—the foresight to map out a safe route escorted by the courage and determination necessary for accomplishing her objective.

REFERENCES

Bremmer, Lawrence M., and Springer, A.: Radical change in counselor education and certification. *The Personnel and Guidance Journal, 49:*94, 1971.

Dudley, Gerald: School counselor certification: A study of current rent requirements. *The School Counselor, 17:,* 1970.

Farmer, Helen S.: Helping women resolve the home-career conflict. *The Personnel and Guidance Journal, 49:,* 1971.

Foster, Charles R.: *Guidance for Today's Schools.* New York, Ginn and Company, 1957.

Horrocks, John E.: *The Psychology of Adolescence.* Boston, HM, 1969.

Hurlock, Elizabeth B.: *Adolescent Development.* New York, McGraw, 1967.

Isaken, Henry L.: Emerging models of secondary counseling as viewed from the context of practice. *The School Counselor, 14:,* 1967.

Locke, Don C.: The "disadvantaged" counselor. *The Guidance Clinic,* March 1973.

Loughary, John W.: To grow or not to grow. *The School Counselor, 18:,* 1971.

Ohlsen, Merle M.: Vocational counseling for girls and women. *The Vocational Guidance Quarterly, 17:,* 1968.

Pogrebin, Lettie Cottin: The working woman: Job counseling. *Ladies Home Journal,* August, 1973.

Scott, C. Winfield: Threads that bind us together. *The Personnel and Guidance Journal, 46:,* 1968.

Smith, Donald Hugh: White counselor in the negro slum school. *The School Counselor, 14:,* 1967.

CHAPTER 12

CAREER ROLES FOR FEMALES
IN THE PHYSICAL SCIENCES

BEATRICE L. SHEPARD

A Candidate for a Scientific Career May Not Even Know What
  Science Is All About
Sometimes the Problem Is Not Actual Discouragement, But
  Lack of Encouragement
Competitive "In-Fighting" Is Just Part of the Game As Far As
  Men In Science are Concerned: They are Experienced,
  Having Done It Among Themselves All Along
A Sense of Humor is Essential
Women Themselves Often Cling to Leftover Prejudices
Beware Those Who Don't Know They Don't Know!

IT MAY BE POSSIBLE to realize some of the immensity of the subject "career roles in the sciences" if we note that the specialties list of the National Register of Scientific and Technical Personnel lists under the categories of biology; chemistry; physics; astronomy, atmospheric, lithospheric and hydrospheric specialties; mathematics; psychology, sociology, anthropology and interdisciplinary specialties; eighty-four "sub-categories, (such as biochemistry, botany, immunology, forestry, organic chemistry, solid state physics, meteorology, psychometrics, topology, educational psychology, demography and population, anthropology) ; and under these subcategories are listed some eleven hundred specialties.

Covering the whole field of science is like covering the whole world! Each one of the categories and each one of the specialties has special requirements in preparation, training, experience, and even aptitude and personality characteristics that should be taken into consideration when planning a career.

It seems that there are two important aspects in career counseling for the sciences, and it is hard to say which is the more important. One is to warn or discourage those with personalities and aptitudes not suited to engaging in scientific pursuits. The other is to encourage in every way possible and to support through discouragements and difficulties those who are interested and have special aptitudes for science. Due to built-in attitudes towards women in science, the second aspect may be more important than the first in the counseling of young women, but a knowledge of the undesirable factors which should warn against a scientific career should also be known and kept in mind.

A CANDIDATE FOR A SCIENTIFIC CAREER MAY NOT EVEN KNOW WHAT SCIENCE IS ALL ABOUT

It is desirable that a young woman interested in a scientific career become as well acquainted with the field and its requirements as possible before college days. There are a number of ways that this can be accomplished. One is to read as widely in the field as possible. Many persons are in the bacteriology field today as a result of reading works by such popularizers of microbial sciences as Paul deKruif with his *Microbe Hunters* and Hans Zinsser with his *Rats, Lice, and History.* Such magazines as *Scientific American* and *Science News* will serve to give a good picture of the world of science and the kind of work interested young readers can look forward to doing.

Some kind of experience in actual scientific laboratories or work projects would be invaluable in determining whether this type of work will be "compatible" with the interested student. This experience may be obtained in many ways. Many schools have science clubs which encourage individual projects and activities among their members. High school science classes require or encourage special science projects from their students. Some schools have established "work-experience" classes where the students engage in specially supervised work in outside scientific laboratories or institutions and receive high school credit for their work. Such a course is contemplated for the Juneau-Douglas High School, in which each student will spend one and one-half hours a day for four weeks in the petro-chemical laboratory of the Federal Bureau of Mines, four weeks in the State Public Health Chemistry Laboratory, and four weeks in the State Public Health Microbiology Laboratory with special work in bacteriology and serology. After an experience like this, the student will have a pretty good idea of whether he or she is interested in following any of these sciences as a career, and the laboratory personnel and high school teachers involved will have a good idea of the capabilities of the students and will be able to give advice and counsel as to future career plans.

Another particular interest of mine has been the encouragement of high school students in trying out laboratory experience as part-time laboratory aides during the school year. We have established a position in the State Public Health Laboratory for one such student who works two hours a day during the school year and full-time on school holidays and during the summer months. A second position has been established to make it possible for us to hire another student, high school or college, for the summer months. During the more than ten years that these positions have been filled, and including special project assistance which we have offered to high school students, we can count twenty-eight students who have come under our "influence." A rough consideration of our experience with this program shows, among those that we still have contact with, three medical technologists, one Ph.D. professor of biochemistry, a second Ph.D. in biochemistry engaged in research, one premedical student, one dentist, one dental hygienist, one science graduate entering nursing, one animal science major, one scientific assistant in a university science department, one psychologist, and one construction engineer. An interesting statistic also emerges: seven of the above are young women. It has been our feeling all along in this program that although we invariably get "more work than we pay for" from these interested young people in their introduction to laboratory work, the most important part of the program is engaging their interests and talents for a future career in science, or, if not in a career, in just knowing and understanding something of what goes on in such fields of endeavor.

SOMETIMES THE PROBLEM IS NOT ACTUAL DISCOURAGEMENT, BUT LACK OF ENCOURAGEMENT

Statistics have shown that by far the greatest percentage of able, talented high school students that do not go on to college are female. Dr. Mary I. Bunting of the Radcliffe Institute, in an address before the American Society for Microbiology in May, 1971, stated that even more distressing than the fact that this happens is that evidently no real effort is made to encourage them to go on. There is evidence that efforts are being made to change the ways of thinking that have allowed this problem to exist without our even being aware of it. The American Society for Microbiology itself has established a Committee on the Status of Women Microbiologists, which held a round-table at the 1971 Annual Meeting, with the rather instructive title, "A Current Problem in Microbiology—Women." Certain items brought out in the discussion included the following: that women scientists are seldom included in the bull-sessions of their male co-workers (it was mentioned that the very term bull-session eliminates women!); that many professional appointments and conferring of honors, etc. are accomplished as a result of "peer-group" elections, and since most of the scientists are men, the peer group tends to perpetuate this situation by voting for more men (an interesting illustration of this might be the election, in 1973, of ninety-five new members to the National Academy of Sciences, of whom four were women) ; women at the annual meeting at which the round-table was held, stated that they felt "lonely" and suggested that more women scientists be invited to convene the scientific sessions.

We may as well face the facts. Women are not particularly wanted in or welcomed into many of the fields of science. This is not to say that they are not working effectively in these fields, because they are. But, since the beginnings of science and technology, it has been pretty much accepted that these fields are for men. Unfortunately, perhaps, women themselves have agreed that science is not for them, and this makes it even more difficult for a scientifically inclined young woman to enter the field.

Many personal experiences with teachers, professors, counselors and fellow students occur to me as I consider the role of counseling young women who are considering entering some scientific field or specialty as a life work. There was, for example, the curious situation in high school where the chemistry teacher was convinced that girls could not understand chemistry, with the exception of herself, that is. She must have consented to allow an exception once in a while, as I was chosen as a member of the school's chemistry team for that year. There was the college zoology professor who had a reputation for "hating females" and who was reputed to have "never given an A to any female in any of his classes." Yet even he had a former student, female, for a lab assistant, an obviously appreciated one, and I am personally aware of at least one female student to whom he gave an "A". There was the vocational counselor my senior year in college, who, taking into account my interests, and I must assume, my sex, said that about the only field he could see for me was clerical. I couldn't type then, and can't yet! And there was the Dean of the Medical School that I wanted to enter who granted me an interview, and told me that there was almost no chance of my being admitted, but that even if I were admitted, every effort would be made to get me to drop out because they did not want me. Nothing personal—"We do not want women in this profession." Having read a good deal about Dr. Elizabeth Blackwell and her adventures in trying to become the first woman doctor in America, I should not have been surprised. But her date was 1849 and this was 1940, and a good many woman doctors later. The Dean did not need to worry, however, as I managed to enter a scientific field which satisfied my needs both to engage in scientific work and to engage in work that was immediately helpful to my fellow beings.

COMPETITIVE "IN-FIGHTING" IS JUST PART OF THE GAME, AS FAR AS MEN IN SCIENCE ARE CONCERNED: THEY ARE EXPERIENCED, HAVING DONE IT AMONG THEMSELVES ALL ALONG.

Problems continued, however. The first week working as public health chemist for a large county, I was surprised with a delivery of seven five-gallon carboys (glass—the days of plastic containers was in the future), three of which contained 200 proof alcohol, two contained distilled water, and the others were empty. In answer to my confused look, the messenger said, "The public health chemist always prepares the denatured alcohol for the entire county."

I did it. I wasn't going to let my five-foot-two femaleness stand out in contrast to my husky six-foor-four male predecessor. It was a trick, siphoning off the correct amounts of alcohol and water, adding the denaturing material, and mixing (did you ever try shaking a full five-gallon glass carboy?) the carboys of alcohol. The challenge was there, even though unspoken: If you want to compete in a world that has been hitherto reserved mainly for males, you can't ask for special conditions.

This, then, is one of the major considerations for a young woman planning to enter a scientific field: You can't ask for special conditions.

A cartoon a few years ago showed Dagwood explaining to Blondie that scientists had discovered that mice were different from men. So, it may seem, are women. This has nothing to do with liberty or talent. There are just differences. The probability of differences is another consideration for a young woman seeking a career in science.

A SENSE OF HUMOR IS ESSENTIAL

One aspect of entering a difficult, competitive field bothers me, and that is what it may do to the individual. The difficulties of competing in a somewhat hostile field, and one which requires exceptional amounts of concentration and whole-hearted dedication, are apt to lead to real personality changes in the individual herself. Without an abundance of such qualities as flexibility, dedication, and a good sense of humor, the individual is apt to become overly hard-nosed, hard-headed, humorless, and, strangely, resentful of and derogatory toward the abilities of other women. It has become the custom to refer to what is a frequent effect on young women's taking on new and difficult experiences in such a field as "culture shock," which develops with frustration, feelings of hostility, and disproportionate anger at seemingly insignificant and trivial occurrences. This may lead to an even more hostile phase where the individual is convinced that the people around her do not understand and do not care, with the resultant feeling that if you make it, you've made it by yourself, and therefore you owe nobody else anything. This phase, which occurs frequently, is not too undesirable if it does not harden into a permanent attitude, or if it does not result in rejection of the entire experience. Confronted with the attitudes of many people in our society, however, that girls should be responsible homebodies, and boys should be independent, self-reliant individuals and that any female who attempts to break out of this mold is "different," it is understandable that a young female "budding scientist" may be tempted to overreact to the point of becoming hostile and aggressive, even perhaps, obnoxious, and it is at this point that counseling and support are important.

This phase, it should be pointed out, often comes as a surprise and unexpectedly, as it usually follows a sort of "honeymoon" period when the individual is exceptionally fascinated and excited over the new experience which she is entering to the point that she does not recognize the tensions and problems which are building up around her. When she becomes aware of the difficulties arising around her, real, and then later, probably also imagined, she will be tempted to give up the struggle or to overreact.

In most instances, this phase ends, or at least comes to the point where it can be coped with. Reading the literature in scientific journals today, however, it becomes apparent that a great proportion of women in science still feel that there are some forms of discrimination in types of assignments, advancement, salary, etc. It is still a quite common feeling that women are fine for most types of routine assignments, but that men are desirable for research projects. And although women are overwhelmingly predominant in medical laboratories, when an administrative or supervisory position is opened up, it is almost invariably filled by a man. Salary surveys have shown that salaries are consistently lower for women in similar positions to men with the same qualifying degrees and experience.

Although much has been said and written to show that much of the so-called discrimination of the forms mentioned are caused by the attitudes and characteristics of the women themselves, this does not completely explain away the situation. It is true that women, after years of preparation and training, do marry, have families and leave the profession, so that work statistics on women show fewer working years, which may also explain lower salaries, less advancement, and reluctance to place "uncertain" persons in positions of administration and supervision. However, statistics are really not that bad and do not seem to justify such attitudes. Also, increasing numbers of well-trained women are, after their families are grown, taking refresher training in their scientific disciplines and re-entering their fields with enthusiasm and greater dependability. There is no question, though, but that we have to function in the presence of accepted and developed attitudes about women, right or wrong.

WOMEN THEMSELVES, OFTEN CLING TO LEFTOVER PREJUDICES

One problem connected with supervisory positions can be traced in many cases to women themselves, in their often expressed feeling that they prefer working for men bosses. This often operates as a boomerang later on when the person who made this observation finds herself being passed over for a supervisory position.

Many people admire Thomas Edison and his many discoveries, but particularly the light bulb. They wish they could do something like that. But very few realize, or would care to go through, all the thousands of unsuccessful or preliminary experiments that

Edison went through before he succeeded in producing one working light bulb. Most scientific pursuits require patient, persistent, often dogged, work to produce the results which may seem spectacular to an outsider. The consideration here is if the passion to know, to discover the answer, is sufficient to overcome impatience with failure and imperceptible results? It's a matter, really, of overwhelming intellectual curiosity which is one of the most important attributes in pursuit of the sciences.

On the other hand, intellectual curiosity uncontrolled or untempered with intellectual honesty (integrity) is dangerous. Many a scientific "discovery" has been achieved as a result of a desire for a result, a desire to "discover" a "predetermined" answer, but with resultant embarrassment when further study by other scientists shows the result to be unrepeatable or unfounded, or founded upon false or carelessly formed premises. It is true that some scientists of stature have made worldwide reputations on work that has later been proved to be mistaken or poorly supported by scientific proof. But ordinarily, forging on to a preconceived result in disregard of the evidence not only leads to poor scientific work habits but is also apt to color the scientist's reputation among her co-workers and the scientific community at large. Intellectual integrity must rank high with the person entering a scientific field.

BEWARE THOSE WHO DON'T KNOW THEY DON'T KNOW!

A few weeks ago I had an unusual opportunity to hire a young girl who offered to go to work for us. Her ambition, she said, was to do research. I asked what her background was, and it came out that she had a high school diploma, one year of college, and a small amount of experience as a clerk-typist. She was tired, she told me, of pushing those papers around, and she had decided she would like to do research. I told her that we were indeed looking for a clerk-typist, and that in that position she would be working with scientific reports and with trained scientific workers and this might satisfy her desire to work in a scientific field. "Oh, no," she assured me, "I want to do research." I told her that I, too, would like to do research, but that I didn't have enough training for it. I'm afraid my humor was completely lost on her. So I told her we had nothing for her unless she wanted to consider the clerk-typist job. As she left, she said airily, "Well, I'll keep you in mind. . ." The young woman seeking to enter a scientific field must recognize the need for adequate training, followed by sufficient experience under good supervision!

Much of the work done in scientific fields, particularly in chemistry and microbiology, involves the handling of dangerous materials: explosives, poisons, corrosive materials, disease-producing bacteria, parasites, fungi, etc. A good, healthy "fear" of the results of careless handling or misuse of these substances is desirable. (I recall a high school student who was quite resentful toward us because we refused to furnish her a chemical which she deemed absolutely essential to a project she wanted to do for her high school biology class. All she wanted was a little arsenic.) Carelessness in protection of one's own self from accident or contamination is very undesirable, but care for the safety of co-workers is also essential. Examples of disregard for laboratory safety are much more frequent, and frightening, than they should be and indicate in some instances lack of training in safety; but in some instances I believe a serious personality characteristic exists that should have ruled out the person as a candidate for any scientific field. Laboratory accidents can occur to the most careful and adept of workers, but every laboratory worker has experienced accident-prone co-workers who are often on the workmen's-compensation rolls for cuts, bruises, burns, and laboratory-acquired infections. One extreme example of disregard for all the rules of laboratory safety was a worker in a bacteriology laboratory who was performing an autopsy on a guinea pig that had been injected with Mycobacterium tuberculosis, the organism causing tuberculosis. One of her co-workers noticed that her fingernails, which were about an inch long, had penetrated her rubber gloves, and were sticking out into her field of work. When this was pointed out to her, she said, "Oh, I'm not afraid." After she finished her work, she walked to the door, turned the knob, walked down the hall, opened another door, and went into another room without removing her gloves. No, she was not afraid, but she left behind her a few that were, and I believe I can safely say that she is not working in a bacteriology laboratory today. A person who is not capable of comprehending the dangers in what she is doing should not be given any encouragement to enter a hazardous occupation. An ability to comprehend the dangers inherent in the work, and a feeling of responsibility for the safety of others, as well as one's self, is an important consideration when going into certain of the scientific specialties.

There are some other considerations which may seem a little "petty," but there is little question that a person who faints at the sight of blood or one who knocks over a glass of milk or a cup of coffee with exceptional frequency has no business working in certain scientific fields which require manual dexterity and personal "balance." Squeamishness, poor coordination, lack of manual dexterity should rule out candidates for medical, biological and chemical fields.

It is frequently said that "attrition" keeps the applicants for scientific fields to a manageable level and screens out the unfit or unsuitable. This means, in a more crude way of speaking, that the young person either drops out or is "flunked" out somewhere during the college training, or even later while working in the field. It is unfortunate that a goodly number of persons, obviously unsuited for scientific professions, get this far before dropping out, and it is to be hoped that with more effective counseling, the number could be reduced.

We can say, then, that these are some of the important considerations that must be made by a young woman considering entering a scientific field.

1. You cannot ask for special conditions just because you are a woman. (On the other hand, you should be able to expect, and should be willing to push for, equal treatment in form of salary, working conditions, advancement, opportunities, etc.)
2. It is necessary to recognize that there are differences between men and women pursuing scientific careers, as in every other career and as in life itself.

3. A young woman entering a scientific field must guard against over reacting to the difficulties and problems, real or imagined, that confront her.
4. The passion to know, or to discover the answer, must be sufficient to overcome impatience with failure and/or imperceptible results. An overwhelming intellectual curiosity is a great scientific attribute.
5. Willingness to work for painstaking accuracy must take precedence over the desire to "finish."
6. Intellectual honesty must control the desire to proclaim results which have not been substantiated by the evidence.
7. It is essential to realize the need for adequate training and experience under good supervision in the chosen field.
8. Comprehension of the dangers in some of the substances handled and desire to protect the safety of others as well as one's self is a fundamental requirement.

Any young woman who can fill these qualifications should be grabbed and held on to and encouraged in every way possible. The field of science needs her!

INDEX

A

Academician, 118
Accounting, 61
Advertising, 61
American Board of Professional Psychology (ABPP), 114
American Dietetic Association, 37
American Institute of Banking (AIB), 67, 73
American Personnel and Guidance Association (APGA), 177
American School Counselor Association (ASCA), 177
American Speech and Hearing Association (ASHA), 104
Applied economics, 55
Association for Counselor Education and Supervision (ACES), 177
Astin, H. S., 4, 15
Austin, Gwendolyn H., v, 132
Automation, 74

B

Bachtold, L. M., 4, 15
Banking, 64
Barclay, William R., 26
Baruch, G., 8, 15
Beshiri, Patricia H., 21, 26
Black educators, 139
Bowers, John Z., 19, 26
Boyer, James B., 145
Bremmer, Lawrence M., 191
Business economist, 57, 59
Business environment, 53
Businesswomen, 50

C

Career decisions, 11
Cartwright, L. K., 6, 15
Chaplaincy, 80
Coker, R. E., 8, 15
Computers and statistics, 61

D

Diet therapy, 28
Dietetics, 27
Dietitian
  administrative, 30
  air force, 32
  army, 31
  clinic, 29
  counseling, 30
  navy, 31
  research, 29, 34
  salary, 163
  sex, 147, 155
  shared, 30
  teaching, 30, 36
  therapeutic, 29
Discrimination, 73, 129
  salary, 163
  sex, 20, 147, 155
Donnelly, T. G., 15
Dudley, Gerald, 191

E

Economic consultants, 58
Economics, 53
Epstein, C. F., 4, 15

F

Farmer, Helen C., 191
Fashion industry, 60
Floyd, Dorothy, B., v, 170
Food technology, 28
Foster, Charles R., 191
Foster, Grace H., v, 64
Fox, D. J., 16

G

Government, 61
Grindle, Evelyn Staples, v, 74
Grumbine, Cecily Anne Gardner, vi, 112

205

Grundy, Betty L., vi, 17
Guidance counseling, 154, 170

H

Helson, R., 15
Hoffman, L. W., 4, 12, 15
Horrocks, John E., 191
Hospital diatetics, 28
Housekeeping, 62
Hurlock, Elizabeth B., 191

I

Industrial psychology, 129
International Association of Women Ministers, 97
Isaken, Henry L., 191

J

Job permanency, 139
Job security, 138

K

Kaplan, H. I., 15

L

Levi, Jr., 16
Locke, Don C., 191
Lopate, Carol, 19, 21, 26
Loughary, John W., 178, 191

M

Mausner, J. S., 15
McKemie-Belt, Virginia Lee, vi, 50
Medical career, 17, 20
Medical specialties, 22
Merchandising, 60
Miller, N., 15
Murdock, Betty, vii, 101

N

National Education Association, 133, 140
National Home Economics Association, 128
National Vocational Guidance Association (NVGA), 177

O

Office management, 61

Ohlsen, Merle W., 191
Orthodontist, 110

P

Parmlee, R. C., 19, 26
Pennell, Maryland Y., 21, 26
Phelps, Charles E., 19, 26
Phillips, B. S., 15
Physical sciences, 192
Pogrebin, Lettie Cottin, 191
Powers, L., 19, 26
Psathas, G., 3, 15
Psychiatrist, 113
Psychologist, 111, 112
  clinical, 119
  community, 119
  consulting, 120
  educational, 121
  engineering, 121
  environmental, 122
  experimental, 123
  industrial, 123
  school, 125
  social, 125
Psychometrics, 124
Public relations, 61
  program, 110
Publishing, 60

R

Rapoports, R., 4, 15
Rapoports, R. N., 4, 15
Reading specialist, 110
Renshaw, Josephine R., 22, 26
Royster, Preston M., vii, 132

S

Salmon, Margaret Belais, vii, 27
Schachter, S., 8, 15
Scott, C. Winfield, 191
Sex-biased curriculum materials, 149
Sex-segregated courses, 150
Sex stereotyping, 149
Shapiro, C. S., 4, 15
Shepard, Beatrice L., viii, 192
Smith, Donald Hugh, 191
Social pressures, 19
Soule, Bradley, viii, 3

Speech
  audiology, 104
  correction, 111
  pathology, 103, 104
  therapist, 110
  therapy, 101
Springer, A., 191
Standley, Kay, viii, 3
Steinman, A., 13, 16
Stibler, B. J., 15

T

Teaching profession, 132
Theoretical economics, 55
Turner, B., 16
Turner, L., 16

W

Weisenfelder, H., 19, 26
Werner, E. E., 4, 15
White, J. J., 16
Williams, P. A., 4, 7, 16
Woman economist, 51
Woman minister, 83, 88
Woman physician, 21
Woman professionals, 8
Women's Liberation Movement, 75
Working women, 8

Z

Zelkovic, A. A., 15